The Firstborn of God

The Birth of Mary's Son, Jesus
Luke 2:1–21

Eugene LaVerdiere, SSS
with Paul Bernier, SSS

LTP
LITURGY
TRAINING
PUBLICATIONS

To Cheryl and Peter LaVerdiere
and their sons, Charles and Kevin

THE FIRSTBORN OF GOD: THE BIRTH OF MARY'S SON, JESUS,
LUKE 2:1–21 © 2007 Archdiocese of Chicago, Liturgy Training
Publications, 1800 North Hermitage Avenue, Chicago IL 60622;
1-800-933-1800, fax 1-800-933-7094, e-mail orders@ltp.org.
All rights reserved. See our Web site at www.LTP.org.

Cover photo © 1994 The Metropolitan Museum of Art,
Rogers Fund, 1905 (05.42)

Printed in the United States of America.

Library of Congress Control Number: 2007931588

ISBN 978-1-56854-609-4
FGBMS

Contents

An Outline
of Luke 2:1–21

INTRODUCTION (2:1–5)

(1) In those days a decree went out from Emperor Augustus that all the world should be registered. (2) This was the first registration and was taken while Quirinius was governor of Syria. (3) All went to their own towns to be registered. (4) Joseph also went from the town of Nazareth in Galilee to Judea, to the city of David called Bethlehem, because he was descended from the house and family of David. (5) He went to be registered with Mary, to whom he was engaged and who was expecting a child.

BODY (2:6–21)

Mary's Son, the Firstborn Son of God (2:6–7)

(6) While they were there, the time came for her to deliver her child. (7) And she gave birth to her firstborn son and wrapped him in bands of cloth, and laid him in a manger, because there was no place for them in the inn.

The Shepherds and the Angels (2:8–14)

(8) In that region there were shepherds living in the fields, keeping watch over their flock by night. (9) Then an angel of the Lord stood before them, and the glory of the Lord shone around them, and they were terrified. (10) But the angel said to them, "Do not be afraid; for see—I am bringing you good news of great joy for all the people: (11) to you is born this day in the city of David a Savior, who is the Messiah, the Lord. (12) This will be a sign for you: you will find a child wrapped in bands of cloth and lying in a manger." (13) And suddenly there was with the angel a multitude of the heavenly host, praising God and saying,

(14) "Glory to God in the highest heaven,
and on earth peace among those whom he favors!"

The Visit of the Shepherds (2:15–20)

(15) When the angels had left them and gone into heaven, the shepherds said to one another, "Let us go now to Bethlehem and see this thing that has taken place, which the Lord has made known to us." (16) So they went with haste and found Mary and Joseph, and the child lying in the manger. (17) When they saw this, they made known what had been told them about this child; (18) and all who heard it were amazed at what the shepherds told them. (19) But Mary treasured all these words and pondered them in her heart. (20) The shepherds returned, glorifying and praising God for all they had heard and seen, as it had been told them.

THE CIRCUMCISION AND NAMING OF JESUS (2:21)

(21) After eight days had passed, it was time to circumcise the child; and he was called Jesus, the name given by the angel before he was conceived in the womb.

Foreword

Before he could complete this manuscript, Father Eugene LaVerdiere became ill with a rare neurological disorder that made it impossible for him to finish. The broad lines were there, his intentions were clear, and much material had been gathered. But he was unable to bring to the whole the clear, trenchant insights for which he was known. That task was left to me as the secondary author.

Father Gene and I were classmates in the seminary and have been friends for over fifty years. I have edited some of his material. I have read all of his books and articles and had many conversations with him on his insights into the scriptures. We discussed the word of God while vacationing together. My relationship with Father Gene gave me the temerity to accept Liturgy Training Publications' request to finish the manuscript.

I changed as little in the manuscript as possible. In areas that were unfinished or incomplete, I was often able to check on what Father Gene had written in other places or recall conversations we had had on the matter. I did the best I could to remain faithful to his thought and the insights that were his—many of which I have made my own over the years.

Years ago, before the 1976 International Eucharistic Congress, I had recommended Gene to Father Dominic Maruca, SJ, to give a weeklong session on the Eucharist to priests in the Philadelphia area. He wrote to me afterward, saying, "You were right; he is an amazing combination of scholarship and pedagogy." That he was. It is fitting that this book is a reflection on the infancy narrative in Luke. The Gospel according to Luke was Father Gene's first love; his doctoral dissertation was on the Resurrection stories in Luke. This book represents the culmination of years of work and reflection for which he became known around the world.

It is my hope that this final offering from Father Gene will prove a source of enlightenment and inspiration for all who ponder the Nativity story in Luke, and who want to penetrate beyond the saccharine piety that too often surrounds this solemnity. Luke was both a master storyteller and theologian. Father Gene helps us to enter the story and make it our own in ever new and fresher ways. For that, God be praised.

Paul Bernier, SSS
Editor, Emmanuel

Acknowledgments

In offering this book, I wish to thank the members of my family: my mother, Gladys LaVerdiere; my sister, Sister Claudette, MM; my brother, Brother Gary, SSS, art director of *Emmanuel* magazine of Eucharistic Spirituality; my brother, Peter, his wife, Cheryl, and my nephews, Charles and Kevin.

In a special way, I thank my religious family, the Congregation of the Blessed Sacrament, particularly my local community serving St. Jean Baptiste Church in New York City. For their constant encouragement and fraternal support, I thank, especially, my provincial superior, Norman Pelletier, SSS; my local superior, Ernest Falardeau, SSS; and the pastor of the parish, Anthony Schueller, SSS.

I am deeply grateful to my sister Claudette for reading my manuscript.

I dedicate *The Firstborn of God: The Birth of Mary's Son, Jesus* to my brother Peter and his family.

Eugene LaVerdiere, SSS
October 18, 2005
Feast of Saint Luke, Evangelist

Introduction

The Gospel accounts of the birth of Jesus by Matthew and Luke are among the most cherished chapters of the New Testament.

In this book, I will present the infancy narrative according to Luke (2:1–21). I will examine the evangelist's introduction (2:1–5), the story of the birth of the "firstborn" son (2:6–7), the arrival of the shepherds, the appearance of the angels (2:8–20), and the circumcision and naming of Jesus (2:21).

Traditionally, we call the gospel stories of Jesus' birth "the infancy narratives," based on the first verse of the Gospel according to Luke: "Since many have undertaken to set down an orderly account (narrative, *diegesin*) of the events that have been fulfilled among us."

We can call them "the Lukan and Matthean infancy narratives," "the gospel infancy narratives," or "the infancy gospels," referring to their gospel purpose. No matter what we call them, we have heard these stories so often from our childhood that we take them and their meaning for granted. As Christians, how well do we understand them?

Particularly at Christmas, we read or listen to the Gospel infancy narratives of the birth of Jesus romantically through our childhood experience. Luke and Matthew wrote the accounts for adult Christians in their communities. We must read or listen to them and reflect on them through the lens of our adult experience, relating them to our faith, charity, hope, and the challenges of Christian life.

The Gospel infancy narratives are both simple and deep. They proclaim the mystery of Jesus as the Savior *(Soter)*, the Lord *(Kyrios)*, as Immanuel *(Emmanouel)*, the Messiah *(Christos)*, and Shepherd of the people Israel *(Poimanei ton laon mou ton Israel)*.

Many years ago on Christmas, I meditated on the infancy gospels through a contemporary Christmas story. The stories challenged me to relate the birth of Jesus to his mission and ministry, even his Passion and Resurrection.

We all have our favorite Christmas stories. One of mine is the farewell gift of Mother Mary Coleman, MM, a gentle woman who spent a good part of World War II in an internment camp of Los Banos in the Philippines. Eventually, Mother Mary Coleman became the dean of Maryknoll Teacher Training College and later Mother General of the Maryknoll Sisters. She was called to God in heaven on April 7, 1984.

"The Japanese guards were kind to us," she told me. "When they had enough to eat, we also had enough. It was only toward the end of the war that they did not have enough.

"We had quite a lot of freedom within the camp. We even had a room set aside for prayer. One of the Filipinos carved a fine wooden crucifix for the room, and we put it up on the wall. The crucifix became a focus for our prayer.

"One of the guards often observed us, careful not to disturb us. The Japanese have a great appreciation for meditation. You can see it in their gardens, many of them just for contemplation. Most, however, know nothing of Christ and his Passion.

"When Christmas came, some Filipinos carved a whole manger set for our prayer room, and we put it out quite early in Advent. Little things, especially religious, symbolic things, mean a lot more when you are interned and have no idea of what may lie ahead.

"When we put out the manger, we did not include the child Jesus during Advent. Then, on Christmas Eve, we had a little ceremony for laying the child in the manger, and we spent some time in prayer.

"Through the Christmas season, we often came to pray before the manger. As we did, the guard who watched us pray before the crucifix observed us even more closely. Once, as some of us were leaving the room, he pointed to Jesus in the manger and then to Jesus on the cross, and asked, 'The same one?' I answered softly, 'Yes, the same one.' Looking again from the manger to the crucifix, he said, 'I am sorry.'"

Mother Mary Coleman's story comes to mind just about every time I read Luke's account of Mary laying her newborn child Jesus in a manger, because there was no room for them in the inn (2:6–7). From New Testament times to our day, few images have had greater influence on the Christian imagination. Few, however, associate the figure of Jesus in the manger with the figure of Jesus on the cross. Neither did those interned at Los Banos until a Japanese guard who did not understand made the connection for them.

We cannot, and need not, divest ourselves of our image of the manger and the way it has been shaped by centuries of art and popular representations. But we can rediscover it and see it anew. We can enrich our popular image through close attention to the story in Luke.

Through the image of the manger, Luke draws readers into a theological motif of rejection and fulfillment. The turning away of the unborn Jesus at the inn of Bethlehem is the first of many times Jesus is refused. Throughout the Gospel, each rejection of Jesus announces the ultimate rejection at Jerusalem and the fulfillment (*ton peplerophoremenon,* 1:1) of Jesus' mission. Everything in the story of Jesus, including his birth, is connected with the Passion and Resurrection. This is what makes Jesus' birth truly Gospel. Apart from the Passion and Resurrection, all that Jesus did and taught—indeed, his very birth—loses its purpose. The Passion and Resurrection bring out the full meaning of Jesus' birth. In more theological terms, the redemption begins with the Incarnation, and the Incarnation is fulfilled in the redemption. Neither is meaningful without the other.

The angel's message to the shepherds announced the Gospel that "to you is born this day in the city of David a Savior, who is the Messiah, the Lord" (2:11). The one born (Incarnation) is a Savior (redemption), the Messiah, the Christ, God's anointed, who would lay down his life, be raised from the dead and revealed as the risen Lord. The angel's message to the shepherds is a synopsis of the Gospel account.

But to see the birth of Jesus as Gospel, we should avoid the expression "glad tidings," which for most of us has little connection with evangelization. The sign of a child lying in a manger is a lot more than "glad tidings."

The Japanese guard in Mother Mary Coleman's story saw the sisters praying before the crucifix and later before the manger. Connecting the child in the manger with the adult crucified, the guard reacted empathetically. He was a good man, but without Christian faith, he could not see the mystery contained in his question: "The same one?" For the faithful, the guard's question bathes the manger with the light of the cross. Like Mother Mary Coleman, we answer with unspeakable joy: "Yes, the same one!"

When we celebrate the birthday of historical persons, we do not celebrate only their birth. We celebrate also their life, their relationships, and their achievements.

At Christmas, we do not celebrate only the birth of Jesus. We rejoice, too, in his life and its relationship to the apostles, disciples, and the assembly. During this joyous time, the mission, ministry, death, and Resurrection of Jesus are not forgotten. They are part of the solemnity, for those events bring meaning to the Nativity.

Without his Passion and his Resurrection, the story of Jesus would not be a Gospel account or Good News for us. Creeds from the early days of the Church, hymns through the centuries, and accounts of the birth of Jesus refer to his Passion and Resurrection.

The following statements from Romans and Philippians provide evidence that the creeds of the early Church spoke in unison of the birth, Passion, and Resurrection of Jesus.

> *(Christ Jesus) was descended* (genomenou, *born) from David according to the flesh and was declared to be Son of God with power according to the spirit of holiness by resurrection from the dead, Jesus Christ our Lord. (Romans 1:3–4)*

> *(Christ Jesus) who, though he was in the form of God* (en morphe theou),
> *did not regard equality with God*
> *as something to be exploited,*
> *but emptied* (ekenosen) *himself,*
> *taking the form of a slave* (morphe doulou),
> *being born* (genomenos) *in human likeness.*
> *And being found in human form* (schmemati hos anthropos),
> *he humbled* (etapeinosen) *himself and became obedient* (hypekoos) *to the point of death—*
> *even death on a cross* (thanatou de staurou). *(Philippians 2:6–8)*

These creedal statements would have been part of the prayer life of Saints Matthew and Luke. As we read the infancy narratives in their accounts of the Gospel, we are taking in the fruit of their contemplation.

The infancy gospels, as well as the prologues of Mark and John, are the gospels in miniature, introducing the principal themes of their Gospel accounts, including the mission, ministry, Passion, and Resurrection of Jesus.

In examining the following passage from Luke's account of the birth of Jesus, we see how the evangelist relays Jesus' mission and relationship to the Church through the infancy narrative. "(She) laid him in a manger *(en phatne),* because there was no place for them in the inn *(en to katalymati)*" (2:7). Mary laid Jesus in a manger, a feeding trough for the animals. In this context, Mary offers Jesus, her son, the firstborn of God, as nourishment for the flock *(epi ten poimnen,* 2:8), because there was no place of hospitality for the son of David (1:32; 2:4) in the city of David (2:4, 6). In Luke, the flock symbolizes the community of disciples and the Christian community. Jesus, we see, addresses his followers as a flock.

> He said to his disciples,
> "Therefore I tell you, do not worry about your life,
> what you will eat, or about your body, what you will wear.
> Do not be afraid, little flock (to micron poimnion),
> for it is your Father's good pleasure
> to give you the kingdom." (12:22, 32)

In the Acts of the Apostles, Christ's followers continue to be addressed as "the flock." The metaphor is expanded as Saint Paul instructs the elders "to shepherd the church of God."

> From Miletus [Paul] sent a message to Ephesus, asking the
> elders of the church to meet him. When they came to him, he
> said to them:
> "Keep watch over yourselves and over all the flock (panti
> to poimnio), of which the Holy Spirit has made you overseers,
> to shepherd (poimainein) the church of God that he obtained
> with the blood of his own Son. I know that after I have gone,
> savage wolves will come in among you, not sparing the flock
> (tou poimniou)." (Acts 20:17, 28–29)

The "inn" *(katalyma),* literally the place of hospitality, foreshadows the "guest room" *(katalyma)* in which Jesus will eat the Passover as the Last Supper with his disciples:

> "Listen," he (Jesus) said to them, "when you have entered the
> city, a man carrying a jar of water will meet you; follow him into

the house he enters and say to the owner of the house, 'The teacher
asks you, "Where is the guest room (to katalyma), *where*
I may eat the Passover with my disciples?"' He will show you
a large room upstairs, already furnished. Make preparations for
us there." (Luke 22:10–12)

At his birth, Jesus was denied hospitality, or rejected by the city of David. In response, Mary, as a symbol of the Church, offers Jesus as nourishment for the flock, that is, the Christian community. At his death, the city of David rejects Jesus. In response, Jesus gave the ultimate hospitality, offering himself as nourishment for the world. In the Gospel according to Luke, the story of Jesus' birth prefigures the story of his Passion and Resurrection.

The account that Matthew presents of the wise men adoring Jesus brings forth images from Isaiah and the psalms.

A multitude of camels shall cover you,
the young camels of Midian and Ephah;
all those from Sheba shall come.
They shall bring gold and frankincense,
(pherontes chrysion kai libanon oisousi)
And shall proclaim the praise of the LORD. *(Isaiah 60:6)*

May the kings of Tarshish and of the isles
render him (God) tribute,
may the kings of Sheba and Seba
bring gifts.
May all kings fall down before him,
all nations give him service
Long may he (God) live!
May gold (chrysion) of Sheba be given to him.
May prayer be made for him continually,
And blessings invoked for him all day long. (Psalm 71:10–15;
Psalm 72:10–11, 15)

In presenting the Magi prostrate before Jesus, Matthew shows the newborn as reigning in the kingdom of heaven through his Passion. Other parts of the visit of the wise men, too, foreshadow the Passion and death of Jesus. To the gifts that the Magi bring, Matthew's addition of myrrh, an ointment for the dead, focuses on the death of Jesus. The question of the wise men in Matthew 2:2 ("Where is the child who has been born king of the Jews?") parallels the query of the governor ("Are you the King of the Jews?") in Matthew 27:11. The question of the wise men also looks to the charge on the cross ("This is Jesus, the King of the Jews") in Matthew 27:37.

Meditations on the Birth of Jesus

Let me describe three presentations of the symbols or images of Jesus' birth:

1. a literary image from a letter of Saint Ignatius of Antioch about the manifestation of the Incarnation;
2. a symbol sculpted in stone on a door lintel in the Royal Portal of the Cathedral of Chartres;
3. a symbolic presentation in a stained glass window, also in the Cathedral of Chartres.

Saint Ignatius of Antioch on the Incarnation

In 108 AD, Saint Ignatius, the third bishop of Antioch, was condemned to be killed by the beasts in the Colosseum. His journey to Rome for the execution took him through churches in Asia Minor. While in Smyrna, he wrote letters to the Ephesians, Magnesians, Trallians, and Romans. When he reached Troas, he wrote to the Philadelphians, Smyrnaeans, and his friend, Saint Polycarp, the bishop of Smyrna.

Each time I read these seven letters I find new images, comparisons, and references to the Christian and Hebrew traditions.

The Pentateuch, the historic and prophetic books, and the books of wisdom all are evident in the writings.

Focusing on the Incarnation, Passion, and Resurrection and its manifestation to the Magi[1] in the Gospel of Matthew 2:1–12 and to the shepherds in the Gospel of Luke 2:8–20, I remembered that Saint Ignatius wrote about the star *(aster)* as a symbol of Jesus. The reference is in the last part of his "To the Ephesians" (XIX), written from Smyrna.

Ignatius starts with a proclamation, announcing:

And the virginity of Mary, and her giving birth were hidden from the Prince of this world as was also the death of the Lord Three mysteries of a cry which were wrought in the stillness of God. (XIX, 1)[2]

Ignatius relates the beginning of the Gospel tradition, the annunciation to Mary and the birth of Jesus to the climax of the Gospel tradition, with the Passion and the Resurrection of Jesus. After proclaiming the three mysteries, Ignatius rhetorically asks, "How, then, were they revealed to the ages?" In other words, "How, then, were the mysteries proclaimed to the world and revealed to Christians like us?"

Ignatius responds:

How then was he manifested to the world? A star shone in heaven beyond all the stars and its light was unspeakable, and its newness caused astonishment, and all the other stars, with the sun and moon, gathered in chorus round this star and it far exceeded them all in its light; and there was perplexity, whence came this new thing, so unlike them. (XIX, 2)

His answer was based on the star of the Magi: "For we observed his star at his rising" (Matthew 2:2). As in Matthew's account, the brilliant star, a symbol of Jesus, outshone others. The other stars were the symbols of the archangels, the saints, and the martyrs. Like the angels, the saints, and the martyrs, all the stars in heaven that surrounded the star of Jesus were worshipping the Lord Jesus. In a few months, as a martyr, Saint Ignatius would join the choir with his predecessors, Saint Peter, the first bishop of Antioch; Saint Evodius, the second bishop of Antioch; and his friend Saint Polycarp.

Ignatius continues the proclamation:

> *By this all magic was dissolved and every bond of wickedness vanished away, ignorance was removed, and the old kingdom was destroyed, for God was manifest as man* (theou anthropinos *[as human form]* phanerou menou) *for the "newness" of eternal life, and that which had been prepared by God received its beginning. Hence all things were disturbed, because the abolition of death was being planned.* [4]

Saint Ignatius may have been reflecting on the choir of angels that joined the angels to the shepherds in the Good News:

> *In that region there were shepherds[5] living in the fields, keeping watch over their flock by night. Then an angel of the Lord stood before them, and the glory of the Lord shone around them, and they were terrified. But the angel said to them, "Do not be afraid; for see—I am bringing you good news of great joy for all the people: to you is born this day in the city of David (Bethlehem) a Savior who is the Messiah the Lord This will be a sign for you: you will find a child wrapped in bands of cloth and lying in a manger." (Luke 2:8–12)*

The angels were praising God at Jesus' birth:

> *And suddenly there was with the angel a multitude of the heavenly host*
> *praising God and saying,*

"Glory to God in the highest heaven,
and on earth peace among those whom he favors!"
(Luke 2:13–14)

In his meditation, Saint Ignatius related the star of the Magi from Matthew to the choir of the shepherds from the Gospel according to Luke. Saint Ignatius of Antioch lived amid the same symbolic world in which the gospel accounts were written. Considering the image of the star, he entered the two stories of Jesus' birth, joining them as one. Inside the Gospel accounts, he meditated on the story when "God was manifest as man (*theou anthropinos* [in human form] *phaneroumenou*)." As were Matthew and Luke, Ignatius was a spiritual and pastoral writer, announcing the Gospel of Jesus' birth.

With our faith imagination, we also can enter the story of Jesus' birth. From inside the Gospel, we can gain fresh insights into the infancy narrative, engaging in a eucharistic contemplation of the Incarnation.

The Cathedral of Chartres on Jesus' Birth

A few years ago, I was teaching a two-week course in Paris. I spent my free days traveling to the Cathedral of Chartres and focusing on the Royal Portal in the west façade in the front of the cathedral.

As had happened to me often in my reading of Luke and Matthew's accounts and the letter of Saint Ignatius of Antioch to the Ephesians, I was surprised during a visit by what I had missed earlier. I had not seen a glaring detail in the door lintel of the Royal Portal!

In the sculpture and the stained-glass windows, the Cathedral of Chartres presents the Bible, interpreting biblical history for the people who lived in the twelfth and the beginning of the thirteenth centuries.

Today, the Cathedral of Chartres is a living Bible in stone and glass, detailing accounts from Genesis to the end of Revelation.

As believers approaching and entering the cathedral, we become integral parts of this Bible.

The Royal Portal of a Door Lintel

The Royal Portal has three doors, constructed in the mid-twelfth century. On my first free day, I focused on the right door, presenting the life of Jesus. On the lintel above the door, I saw four scenes sculpted in stone.

Scene One. On the left, the angel Gabriel stands with Mary. The angel's right hand is raised in greeting. Mary appears to be listening. At the feet of the angel, a book of the scriptures is open. The scene illustrates the Annunciation (Luke 1:26–38).

Scene Two. As Mary and Elizabeth stand close together, Mary's right hand grasps Elizabeth's left hand. It conjures an image of the New Testament (Mary) reaching out to the Old Testament (Elizabeth). The scene evokes Luke's story of Mary's song of praise during the visitation (1:46–55).

Scene Three. On the far right, the angel that announced the Good News of the birth of Jesus to the shepherds is standing:

> *Do not be afraid; for see—I am bringing you good news of great joy for all the people: to you is born this day in the city of David a Savior, who is the Messiah, the Lord. This will be a sign for you: you will find a child wrapped in bands of cloth and lying in a manger. (Luke 2:10–12)*

The shepherds are leading their flocks to Mary's child. The scene portrays Luke's story of the angelic annunciation to the shepherds (2:8–20).

Scene Four. In the middle of the lintel, Mary is lying on a low bed or couch. Behind Mary's bed is a table, on which the Christ child, wrapped in swaddling bands, is lying. Joseph is standing at Mary's head, looking on. In the Cathedral of Chartres, Jesus' manger became an altar table, relating the Incarnation to the Eucharist. The scene depicts the account in Luke of Mary's giving birth to Jesus (2:6–7).

Seeing that excited me. People of the twelfth century understood the story of Jesus' birth in the Gospel according to Luke: "While they were there, the time came for her to deliver her child. And she gave birth to her firstborn son . . . (literally, to her son, the first-born, that is, the firstborn of God!)" (2:6–7a).

As did every other mother in the eastern Mediterranean, Mary wrapped her child in swaddling clothes (2:7b). But, unlike every other mother, Mary swaddled the firstborn of God, presenting the child as just like us, human and mortal.

Mary "laid him in a manger." That is, she offered her son, the firstborn of God, as nourishment for the flock, "because there was no place for them in the inn," no place in the hospitality of the city of David. In the Cathedral of Chartres, Mary laid her son, the first-born of God, on an altar table, evoking Jesus' Last Supper *(to katalyma)*, the guest room, (Luke 22:11) and the Lord's Supper (Luke 22:15–18, 19–20).

The Royal Portal of a Stained-Glass Window

As I entered the cathedral, I saw the scene repeated in a stained-glass window above the same door of the sculpted lintel. Like the Royal Portal, the Incarnation window was also made in the mid-twelfth century, but it has more details, especially in the frame of the birth of Jesus that connects the story in the accounts of Luke and Matthew.

I began to "read" the stained glass window where the story starts with three scenes at the base: the annunciation to Mary on the left, the visitation to Elizabeth in the middle, the Incarnation on the right, and the annunciation to the shepherds on the left above the annunciation to Mary.

Panel One. On the left, in the annunciation to Mary, the angel Gabriel is shown walking to Mary, with the right arm and two fingers raised in salutation. Mary has risen from her seat; her bodily movement expresses astonishment (Luke 1:26–38).

Panel Two. In the middle is the visitation. The angel Gabriel announced that Mary's relative, Elizabeth, "in her old age has also conceived a son" (Luke 1:36a). So Mary comes to the house of Zechariah, enters it, and salutes Elizabeth, six months with child (Luke 1:36b). Elizabeth stands in a red tunic with parted hands, and Mary stands in a green tunic with the left arm raised to greet her older relative (Luke 1:39–56; Mary's Song of Praise [Magnificat]).

Panel Three. On the right is the Incarnation. As on the door lintel, Mary is lying on a low couch. In a partially reclining position, she points to the child Jesus wrapped in swaddling bands on the altar table.

At his birth, the child Jesus is placed not in a homely manger but sacramentally on an altar, here represented by a flat-topped table and supported by two sculpted artistic columns. This symbolizes that body and blood, the *corpus verum* (true body) are present in the Eucharist. As written in the *glossa ordinaria,* a tenth-century compilation of the biblical commentaries of the Church Fathers used widely in the monastic and cathedral schools: "The cradle in which He sleeps is the very altar of sacrifice."

Above the altar are blue-and-white parted curtains, with a lighted sanctuary lamp in between. At the upper right corner of the panel is the shining star that led the Magi to the home of Mary and Joseph (Matthew 2:1–2, 7, 9–10).

Mary rests on a couch, covered with a blue wrapping; the child Jesus is also swaddled in blue. Behind the child on the altar, an ox and ass are presented worshipping their Lord.

The images of the ox and the ass refer to the introduction of Isaiah:

Hear, O heavens, and listen, O earth:
for the LORD *has spoken:*
　I reared children and brought them up,
　　but they have rebelled against me.
The ox knows its owner,
　and the donkey (ass) its master's crib;
but Israel does not know,
　my people do not understand. (Isaiah 1:2–3)

Through Isaiah 1:2–3, the ox and the ass are telling symbols, interpreting the story of Jesus' birth in the Gospel according to Luke: "and (she) wrapped him in bands of cloth, and laid him in a manger, because there was *no place for them in the inn*" (Luke 2:7). We saw this in the Royal Portal as well. In the stained-glass window of the right panel, the images of the ox and the ass connect the Incarnation to the Eucharist as a sacrament of Jesus' redemptive sacrifice.

Joseph is sitting at Mary's feet, sleeping, perhaps dreaming of the angel of the Lord who appeared to him, announcing the good news of the Incarnation:

and (an angel of the Lord) said, "Joseph, son of David, do not
be afraid to take Mary as your wife, for the child conceived
in her is from the Holy Spirit. She will bear a son, and you are
to name him Jesus, for he will save his people from their sins."
All this took place to fulfill what had been spoken by the Lord
through the prophet:

"Look, the young woman is with child and shall bear a son, and
shall name him Emmanuel." (Isaiah 7:14)

The stained-glass window in the third panel of the Royal Portal is thus an artistic synthesis interpreting the birth of Jesus according to the accounts in Luke and Matthew.

Panel Four. The annunciation to the shepherds constitutes the fourth panel, placed directly above the annunciation to Mary.

The angel said, "In that region there were shepherds living in the fields, keeping watch over their flock by night" (Luke 2:8).

All three shepherds wear short peasant medieval smocks and have crooks. Between them, the dogs and masters look upward in astonishment at the swooping angels, who reveal to them that there was "born this day in the city of David a Savior (Jesus), who is the Messiah (Christ), the Lord" (Luke 2:11). The people gazing at these windows in the Middle Ages (and now!) were thus invited to join the shepherds in awe and gratitude when recalling how God so loved the world that he sent his Son to be its salvation and food for life's journey.

Reflection on the Incarnation

Jesus of Nazareth was born in the city of David, Bethlehem, more than two thousand years ago. From the beginning and throughout the history of the Church, Christians have reflected on the birth of Jesus. The reflections of the Gospel accounts, of Saint Ignatius of Antioch, and the builders of the Cathedral of Chartres are still with us.

Continuing the tradition of meditating on the Incarnation, Pope John Paul II promulgated "The Mystery of the Incarnation" *(Incarnationis Mysterium)* in 2000.

> *For two thousand years, the Church has been the cradle in which Mary places Jesus and entrusts him to the adoration and contemplation of all peoples. In the sign of the consecrated Bread and Wine, Christ Jesus risen and glorified, the light of the nations (cf. Luke 2:32) reveals the enduring reality of his Incarnation.* (Incarnationis Mysterium, #11)

On Holy Thursday, April 17, 2003, Pope John Paul II, in the twenty-fifth year of his Pontificate, gave at the Basilica of Saint Peter in Rome, the encyclical letter "On the Eucharist in its Relationship to the Church" *(Ecclesia de Eucharistia):*

In a certain sense Mary lived her Eucharistic faith *even before the institution of the Eucharist, by the very fact that she offered* her virginal womb for the Incarnation of God's Word. *The Eucharist, while commemorating the passion and resurrection, is also in continuity with the incarnation. At the Annunciation Mary conceived the Son of God in the physical reality of his body and blood, thus anticipating within herself what to some degree happens sacramentally in every believer who receives, under the signs of bread and wine, the Lord's body and blood. (*Ecclesia de Eucharistia, *#55)*

As did the writers of the accounts of Luke, Matthew, and John, Saint Ignatius of Antioch, the designers and artists of the Cathedral of Chartres, and Pope John Paul II, we too must meditate on the birth of Jesus. With the help of our rich tradition, we can interpret the stories of Jesus' birth in Luke and Matthew to link Mary's offering Jesus to the world as nourishment with the eucharistic banquet.

1. *The Apostolic Fathers,* translation of English, Kirsopp Lake, (Cambridge, Massachusetts: Harvard University Press, 1959), The Loeb Classical Library, 2 volumes, 1, Ignatius to the Ephesians, 192–193.

2. Ibid.

3. Ibid.

4. Raymond E. Brown, SS, *The Birth of the Messiah,* New Updated Edition (New York: Doubleday, 1977, 1993), 420–424, 672–675.

5. *Symbolism of the Shepherds.* Symbols of rustic virtues for sinners or those outside the Law for the poor, either financially or in spirit, such as the *anawim* for the apostles or church pastors of Davidic background and David was a shepherd in the Bethlehem area when he was called by Samuel to be anointed king (1 Samuel 16), 672–674.

Emperor Augustus and Quirinius, Governor of Syria, and Joseph and Mary

*In those days a decree went out from Emperor Augustus
that all the world should be registered. This was the first registration
and was taken while Quirinius was governor of Syria. All went
to their own towns to be registered. Joseph also went from the town
of Nazareth in Galilee to Judea, to the city of David called
Bethlehem, because he was descended from the house and family
of David. He went to be registered with Mary, to whom he was
engaged and who was expecting a child. (Luke 2:1–5)*

The account Luke provides of the birth of Jesus is simple.
He lays out the setting and the introduction (2:1–5), tells the
event of the birth (2:6–7), announces it as Good News *(euaggeli-
zomai)* of the Savior *(soter),* who is the Messiah *(Christos,* Christ), the
Lord *(kurios)* (2:8–20), and calls Jesus, "the name given by the angel
(Gabriel) before he was conceived in the womb (Mary)" (2:21).

We have heard this story so often that we take it for granted,
as though it were quite ordinary to date the birth of a child by an
imperial decree of the emperor *(para Kaesaros,* of Caesar) and give
the place of birth as the city of David, Bethlehem. We do not even
wonder about laying a newborn, let alone a son of royal lineage of
David (3:31), in a feeding trough, nor about the angel of the Lord

appearing to shepherds living in the fields outside Bethlehem, nor of the son being circumcised and named Jesus.

Once a year, however, we do not take the Gospel account for granted. At Christmas, we gather for midnight Mass to hear the story and celebrate the birth of Jesus. The priest begins, "The Lord be with you," separating it from secular and commercial concerns and the festival outside.

The Good News of Jesus' birth is about to be announced: "In those days a decree *(dogma)* went out from Emperor Augustus that all the world *(pasan ten oikoumenen)* should be registered" (2:1). The reading continues: "This was the first registration *(apographe)* and was taken while Quirinius was governor of Syria" (2:2). As the story of the birth of Jesus is proclaimed at midnight Mass, the assembly is still.

We are there, two thousand years ago, affected by the same decree, setting out for the city of David. Or better, the decree is now, two thousand years later, when over and over again, there is no place in the inn. Every Christmas, the story works its magic, attuning the assembly to the mystery of Christ, recalling Christmases, both personal and historical, from when Mary "gave birth to her firstborn son" (2:7).

At Christmas, we best appreciate the simplicity of the account of the birth of Jesus as poetry. Every phrase, indeed every word, resonates biblically, evoking figures, places, and events from Israel's sacred history, now fulfilled in the birth of Jesus, Mary's firstborn son, a Savior who is Messiah, the Lord (2:11).

Luke relates his account visually. It appears on the canvas of our Christian imagination, formed by years of living the faith. The evangelist's presentation of the event invites us to see as the shepherds saw and celebrated the birth. For this we must have eyes of faith. Even more, we need to have eyes of contemplative faith, taking time to look, be taken in, and become part of what we observe. Even for those who have eyes to see, it requires time to really see.

To receive the full impact of Luke's account, we could start with the annunciation to Zechariah of the conception and birth of John the Baptist. John was a prophet whose life and mission, including his extraordinary birth, was "to turn the hearts of parents to their children, and the disobedient to the wisdom of the righteous, to make ready a people prepared for the Lord" (1:17). The birth of Jesus was the event in Israel's history that brought the mission of John to a climax.

Or we could begin with the annunciation by the angel Gabriel to Mary of the imminent conception and birth of Jesus. The Nativity was an event in divine history, fulfilling the kingdom of Israel in the kingdom of God. The son of Mary will be great *(megas)* and called the Son of the Most High *(hypsistou):* "the Lord God will give to him the throne of his ancestor David *(Dauid tou patros autou,* of David his father). He will reign over the house of Jacob forever *(eis tous aionas),* and of his kingdom there will be no end *(ouk estai telos)*" (1:32–33). This book, however, will limit itself to the narration of the Nativity, as there is more than enough for meditation here.

A Decree of the Emperor Augustus (Luke 2:1)

We will start with the setting for the birth of Jesus with the decree of Emperor Augustus that all the world should be registered (Luke 2:1).

"In those days *(Egeneto de en tais hemerais ekeinais [tautais],*" 2:1; 1:39) is making reference to "In the days *(en tais hemerais)* of King Herod of Judea" (1:5). "A decree *(dogma,* edict, rule, law, order) went out *(exelthen)* from Emperor Augustus *(para Kaisaros Augustou)* that all the world *(pasan ten oikoumenen)* should be registered *(apographesthai,* censused, enrolled)" (2:1).

Luke employed *dogma,* using the technical word in classical Greek "to denote an 'opinion' (what *seems,* from *dokein),* and by extension even a philosophical 'notion.'"[1] The word *dogma* was used especially in the consultation of the Roman Senate *(romanum sena-tus consultum)*, "as distinct from *psephisma,* a vote of the assembly of the people."[2]

Augustus (*Augoustos* in Latin [but transliterated in Luke 2:1], *Sebastos* in Greek), also known as Caesar Augustus, was the first Roman emperor (27 BC–14 AD). He administered and centralized the power of the Roman Empire of his day in Rome and stabilized and secured the *Pax Romana* (Roman Peace). In 13 BC, he erected the *Ara Pacis* (Altar of Peace) on the embankment of the Tiber River and celebrated the peace he had established.

"All the world (pasan ten oikoumenen)" was the Greek *oik-oumene,* meaning "the inhabited earth." It (all the world) was meant to include Italy and the provinces. No evidence exists that it desig-nated only the latter, as distinct from Italy, much less Palestine alone.[3]

The Registration of Quirinius, Governor of Syria (Luke 2:2)

"This the *(he)* first registration (*aute apographe,* [in Latin, *census*]; *prote* [first] *egeneto* [was])" is awkward Greek and should probably read "This first census was under. . . . And it was taken while Quirinius was governor of Syria (*hegemoneuontos* [being in charge] *tes Syrias Kyreniou*)" (2:2b).

Publius Sulpicius Quirinius was a legate of the emperor Augustus in the imperial province of Syria, who also assumed con-trol of Judea.

He was one of the most effective and influential men in Rome. Named governor of Syria in 6 AD, Quirinius was given the responsibility of restructuring Judea after it was annexed to Syria as a Roman province. Quirinius' census was taken up shortly after he took over in 6–7 AD. It was limited to Judea.[4]

The census in Luke that brought Joseph and Mary to Bethlehem has been the source of great historical difficulty, inasmuch as we have no evidence of such a census. Luke situates Jesus' birth in the latter days of the reign of Herod while Quirinius was legate in Syria. There are ten years between the end of the reign of Herod the Great (4 BC) and Quirinius' assumption of power over Judaea (6 AD). The census that Quirinius took up shortly thereafter is well attested historically, especially since an uprising followed it. If this is the census to which Luke refers, it would have taken place years after the birth of Jesus. As far as we know, there was no universal census taken when Luke specified.

Joseph Fitzmyer, SJ, does not see a way to reconcile the data to support a census at Jesus' birth. He states that "Publius Sulpicius Quirinius' career is fairly well-known and defies all attempts to attribute to him two censuses in Judea or to date the start of his legateship of Syria to any other period than AD 6–7 . . . ."[5]

Because there is no reason to doubt that Jesus was born while Herod the Great was still alive, unanswered is the question of why Luke wrote as he did. Three possibilities are worth considering. The first is that he had wrong historical data. Two major revolts occurred around the time of the birth of Jesus. The first was at the end of Herod's life and the second at the time of the annexation of Judea, when the census would have taken place. Luke, who was writing perhaps 75 years later, yet aware of these two periods of upheaval, simply confused the time of the census.

Second, Luke surely conceived and presented Luke-Acts as a work of Christian history. He approached writing his account from a historical viewpoint, and history from a Gospel viewpoint. Luke is careful to situate Jesus in human history, showing his relationship to the Roman world and its provinces as well as providing the grounds for the journey of Mary and Joseph to Bethlehem.

The clearest indications we have of his historical intent might be seen in the two prefatory statements that Luke begins both his account of the Gospel and the Acts of the Apostles. Their form corresponds to the primary and secondary prefaces long employed by Hellenistic historians. This enabled his readers to see how the Gospel could be at home in a Hellenistic culture. It also showed how Hellenistic culture could thrive in a world infused by the Gospel. Those who heard Luke's account also would be able to situate their history as part of a broader history, all of which was determined by God to bring about our salvation by means of "the events that have been fulfilled among us" (Luke 1:1).

Third, Luke may have been a historian in intent, and history in those days was not written with the factual precision demanded today, but he was primarily a theologian. As our examination of the infancy narrative will show, a theological intent is within every detail. Stripped of theological perspective, little would remain of Luke's account, and its narrative form and historical design would be unrecognizable. Luke's theology drives the narrative, with an intention to make us appreciative of how God has acted in history.

Each to His Own City (Luke 2:3)

"All went to their own towns to be registered" (2:3). The demand that each person go to his native place to be registered was contrary to Roman custom, which based the tax on the residence rather than ancestry.[6] In *Roman Civilization, Sourcebook II: The Empire*, we find the introduction of the taxation, the census and the poll tax:

> *The periodicity and procedures of the census varied with the*
> *historical background of the province. . . . The rate of the tax*
> *varied, townspeople, for example, paying less than villagers.*
> *Slaves were included in the declarations and paid for by their*
> *owners at the same rate as they paid for themselves.*[7]

Because we have no evidence of any Roman practice of registering people in their town of origin, registration was usually in the town or city where the tax would be collected. Most commentators today assume that the "registration" was a device Luke used to solve the problem of getting Joseph and Mary from Nazareth, where he assumed they were living, to Bethlehem. From a historical viewpoint, Luke's account is difficult. It is not supported by known facts and is opposed to Matthew's account, which assumes that Joseph and Mary were living in Bethlehem and went to Nazareth in Galilee because Archelaus had begun to reign in Judea.

From a theological viewpoint, however, we can understand Luke's account. Convinced that Jesus was born in Bethlehem, the evangelist assumed that what brought Mary and Joseph there was Quirinius' census. And how else could this have happened if people were not required to go to their ancestral town? The Bethlehem connection also serves to highlight the Davidic origins of Jesus and to alert Luke's readers that Jesus is the fulfillment of the prophecies that the line of David would not die out.

Joseph Goes from Nazareth to Bethlehem (Luke 2:4)

"Joseph also *(kai)* went *(anebe)* from the town of Nazareth in Galilee *(apo tes Galilaias)* to Judea *(eis ten Ioudaian)*, to the city of David *(eis polin Dauid)* called Bethlehem *(hetis kaleitai Bethleem)*, because he was descended of the house and family of David *(kai patrias Dauid)*."

Luke speaks of Nazareth as a town: "In the sixth month the angel Gabriel was sent by God to a town in Galilee called Nazareth" (1:26); "Joseph also went up from the town of Nazareth in Galilee, to the city of David called Bethlehem, because he was descended from the house and family of David."(2:4); "When they had finished everything required by the law of the Lord, they returned to Galilee, to their own town of Nazareth" (2:39); and

"They got up, drove him out of the town, and led him to the brow of the hill, so they might hurl him off the cliff." (4:29).

Distinctions among cities, towns, and villages were not that hard and fast then, and the terms sometimes were used interchangeably. There is no doubt, however, that Luke wanted to highlight the importance of Nazareth. But the town is not referred to before Roman times, and it is more likely that it was a sleepy little village, a few miles south of Sepphoris, a far larger and important city.

Luke refers to Bethlehem as a city *(polis):* "to the city *(eis polin)* of David, called Bethlehem (2:4). In the Gospel according to John, Bethlehem is referred to as a village *(kome):*

> *Has not the scripture said that the Messiah is descended from David and comes from Bethlehem, the village* (apo Bethleem tes komes) *where David lived? (7:42)*

Although Luke does not associate Bethlehem with any prophetic text, the birth of Jesus in Bethlehem is interpreted by Matthew 2:5 as fulfilling the prophecy of Micah 5:2:

> *But you, O Bethlehem of Ephrathah,*
> *who are one of the little clans of Judah,*
> *from you shall come forth for me*
> *one who is to rule in Israel.*

Matthew, however, changes the first line to "Bethlehem of Judea," making the connection that Jesus descended from Judah.

After the census, Joseph went "to the city of David called Bethlehem, because he was descended from the house and family of David" (2:4). This final phrase is intended to emphasize Jesus' Davidic descent, rather than (as some have held) that Joseph had a house or property somewhere in Bethlehem.[8]

Despite attempts to make both Joseph and Mary of the line of David, efforts of a much later tradition, Luke does not know Mary as descended from David. Jesus' descent from David is clearly traced by Luke as being through Joseph:

> *Jesus (Iesous), was about thirty years old when he began his work. He was the son (as was thought) of Joseph son of Heli (3:23) . . . son of Melea, son of Menna, son of Mattatha, son of Nathan, son of David, son of Jesse, son of Obed, son of Boaz. (3:31–32)*

Matthew's account is in agreement with Luke's in tracing Jesus' descent through Joseph (1:16), who is said to be "son of David . . . son of Abraham." Luke goes two steps further in his genealogy, however, by saying that Joseph is "son of David . . . son of Adam . . . son of God" (3:38).

Mary Was with Child (Luke 2:5)

And so, when Quirinius was governor of Syria, the Gospel tells us that Joseph went "to be registered with Mary, to whom he was engaged and who was expecting a child" (2:5). Mary was betrothed to Joseph. Luke never calls her the wife *(gyne)* of Joseph. Fitzmyer suggests that Luke would probably have used that term if he had been aware of Palestinian Jewish marriage customs.[9] Matthew, perhaps more familiar with these customs, reads, "Joseph the *husband (ton andra)* of Mary" (1:16). And again, "When his mother Mary had been engaged *(mnesteutheises)* to Joseph, but—before they lived together *(prin e synelthein autous,* they married) . . . her husband . . . took her as his wife *(ten gynaika autou)*" (Matthew 1:18, 19, 24,). The angel that appeared to Joseph in a dream told him, "Joseph, son of David, do not be afraid to take Mary as your wife for the child conceived in her is from the Holy Spirit" (Matthew 1:20).[10]

Marriages at that time were a two-step process: a formal exchange of consent before witnesses by both families, and the taking of the betrothed to the groom's home, sometimes years later.

This may have originated because girls could be betrothed when they were rather young, and the couple would not begin to live together until much later. During this interval, however, one betrothed was legally considered a man's wife, and the husband had legal claims over her.

Mary, "who was expecting a child," Luke tells us (2:5c) accompanied Joseph on the trip to Bethlehem. Fitzmyer notes that "the phrase, 'who was pregnant,' does not give a reason for Mary's accompanying Joseph; it simply states her condition and prepares for the coming of Jesus in Bethlehem." It was necessary that she accompany Joseph, for her child was to be born in Bethlehem.

Reflection on the Emperor Augustus, Quirinius, and Joseph and Mary

We will start with the setting for the birth of Jesus in the city of David, Bethlehem, as a result of the decree of Emperor Augustus that all the world should be registered (2:1).

When the Annunciation was made to Mary that she would be the mother of the Lord, the most powerful man in the world was Caesar Augustus, emperor of Rome. Under his rule the very name of Rome meant wealth, power, and authority. He had ushered in a reign of peace that lasted almost 50 years. Yet, Luke tells us, his decreeing a census set in motion events that would result in the birth of a child in Bethlehem who would be king of kings and lord of lords.

In the eyes of God, the insignificant couple—as far as the world was concerned—were key players in the history of salvation. There is a certain irony here, and also more than a suggestion that we begin, like Mary, who "treasured all these things in her heart" (2:51b), to learn to see God's action in history. Salvation takes place in the warp of human history, but only for those who are attuned to God's ways.

Quirinius also was a man of stature. He ruled that part of the world where Jesus was born. His census spawned an uprising that he put down summarily. Even though it seems that he was not yet in charge of Judea at the time of the birth of Jesus, Luke situates the birth with him and Augustus to let us see where true greatness lies. "A decree went forth." But God also had a decree: "God sent his Son," Saint Paul tells us (Galatians 4:4). And Saint John reminds us that "God so loved the world that he gave his only Son so that everyone who believes in him may not perish but may have eternal life" (3:16). It is God who controls history.

The birth and childhood of Jesus in the Gospel according to Luke is presented exclusively through Mary (1:5—2:52). Gabriel's annunciation to Mary is followed by Mary's visit to Elizabeth and Song of Praise, the Magnificat. It is Matthew who gives Joseph a more consciously active role. For Luke, Joseph makes it possible for Mary to go to Bethlehem. But it is Mary, who from the beginning was able to say, "Here I am, the servant of the Lord; let it be with me according to your word" (Luke 1:38), who remains our model of how to be an instrument in the hand of God. Openness to the will of God allows one to play a key role in salvation history.

It is also relevant that the birth of Jesus would take place in Bethlehem, the house of bread. In the first prayer that Jesus taught his disciples, he instructed that they should ask God to "give us each day our daily bread." The true bread that Jesus would one day give us is already foreshadowed in his birth and the manger in which he was laid. It is in the Eucharist that we can find the hospitality denied Jesus at Bethlehem, but which he extended to us from the upper room where he gave his body and blood to be food and nourishment on our pilgrim way.

1. Joseph A. Fitzmyer, SJ, *The Gospel according to Luke I–IX,* The Anchor Bible 28 (Garden City, New York: Doubleday and Company, Inc., 1981) 399, note 2:1, *an edict happened to be issued.* Literally, it is "and it happened in those days (that) an edict went forth."

2. R. E. Brown, *The Birth of the Messiah* (A Commentary on the Infancy Narratives in the Gospels of Matthew and Luke), New Updated Edition, The Anchor Bible Reference Library (New York: Doubleday, 1977, 1993) 394, note of Luke 2:1.

3. Brown also suggests that the reader see Acts 11:28 for a similar Lukan usage of "all the world."

4. According to Josephus (Jewish Antiquities), Quirinius takes a census in Syria:

   Now the territory subject to Archelaus was added to (the province of) Syria, and Quirinius, a man of consular rank, was sent by Caesar (Augustus) to take a census of property in Syria and to sell the estate of Archelaus (XVII, xiii, 4).

   Josephus, Jewish Antiquities, translation of English by Ralph Marcus (Cambridge, Massachusetts: Harvard University Press, 1963), The Loeb Classical Library, 9 volumes, Books XV–XVII, 536–537.

5. J. A. Fitzmyer, *The Gospel according to Luke I–IX,* 402. Fitzmyer has several pages trying to sort out the various explanations given.

6. I. Howard Marshall, *Gospel of Luke, A Commentary on the Greek Text, The New International Greek Testament Commentary,* 3 (Grand Rapids, Michigan: William B. Eerdmans Publishing Company, 1978), 101–102 (Luke 2:3).

7. *Roman Civilization, Sourcebook II: The Empire,* edited with an introduction and notes by Naphtali Lewis and Meyer Reinhold, Harper Torchbook, The Academy Library (New York: Harper & Row, Publishers, 1966), *Taxation: Census and Poll Tax,* 388 (The Census in Judaea, Edict of the Prefect of Egypt, A Census Declaration, 388–390).

8. R. E. Brown, *The Birth of the Messiah* (A Commentary of the Infancy Narratives in the Gospels of Matthew and Luke), New Updated Edition, The Anchor Bible Reference Library (New York: Doubleday, 1977, 1993), 396, note of Luke 2:4, *"of the house and lineage of David."*

9. Joseph A. Fitzmyer, SJ, 407.

10. R. E. Brown translates this sentence thus rather than what we find in the NRSV, "to take Mary *as* your wife." Brown explains that in the Jewish understanding of the marital procedure, Mary was already considered to be Joseph's wife, even though they had not yet come together to share bed and board. See p. 129. A more detailed explanation of these customs is found on pp. 123–124.

Mary's Son, the Firstborn Son of God

While they were there,
the time came for her to deliver her child.
And she gave birth to her firstborn son
and wrapped him in bands of cloth,
and laid him in a manger, because
there was no place for them in the inn.
(Luke 2:6–7)

This passage, one sentence in the Greek, is a theological gold mine through which Luke incorporates much of his theology. In the previous verse, Luke tells us that Mary and Joseph lived in Nazareth. This was their hometown. Here, Luke differs from Matthew, who writes that Joseph and Mary were from Bethlehem. In his narrative, Matthew tells us that, after being warned in a dream not to stay in Bethlehem, Joseph moves the Holy Family to Nazareth. No matter what, after the birth of Jesus, Joseph and Mary settled in Nazareth, and it is in Nazareth that Jesus would grow up.

While They Were There (Luke 2:6a)

In the account by Luke, Joseph and Mary travel from Nazareth to Bethlehem, the "city of David," to fulfill the decree of Caesar Augustus that people be counted for a census "each in his own city." Joseph, we are told, "was descended from the house *(ex oikou)* and family *(patrias,* lineage) of David" (Luke 2:4c). In this we can sense an apologetic note: Jesus Christ may have been a king of the ancient dynasty of David, but his reign was not a revolutionary threat to the rule of Caesar Augustus.

This issue will be brought up again in the account of the Passion, when the son born to David's lineage was about to die under Pilate, the Roman prefect of Judea. The soldiers jeered and offered sour wine to Jesus as he hung on the cross: "If you are King of the Jews, save yourself!" (Luke 23:37). Jesus' mission, however, was not to save himself but to save others by laying down his life for them. He would not drink of the fruit of the vine until the kingdom of God was made present in the Lord's Supper: "And he did the same with the cup after supper, saying, 'This cup that is poured out for you is the new covenant in my blood' (22:20). Yet the inscription above Jesus on the cross truly stated, "This is the King of the Jews" (23:38).

Bethlehem, of course, is the place associated with David as the place of his birth. In both the Old and New Testaments, however, it was not called the city of David. Jerusalem, which David conquered and made his capital, was the city of David. Luke's readers must have known this. But by calling Bethlehem the city of David in the prologue, Luke evokes the end of Jesus' life journey in Jerusalem, where he would be rejected, just as he had been in Bethlehem.

Mary Delivered Her Child (Luke 2:6b)

While Joseph and Mary were in the city of David, Bethlehem, the time came for her to deliver her child. The expression Luke used for "the time came," was literally, "the days were fulfilled" *(eplesthesan hai hemerai,* 2:6b). Mary's child was at the center of Luke's general theme of the promise and fulfillment that governed events in the history of salvation. The birth of Jesus was the most important event in the history of salvation. Ultimately, God's promise of salvation would be fulfilled though Jesus.

The announcement by the angel Gabriel that Mary would bring forth a son who would be called Son of the Most High, and to whom the Lord God would give the throne of his ancestor David, was fulfilled. Mary had placed herself at the disposition of the Lord, accepting that all be done as Gabriel had announced, for nothing was impossible for God. Scripture is filled with examples of how God did the seemingly impossible. The words of Gabriel recall the announcement to Abraham that Sarah would conceive and bring forth a son:

> The LORD said to Abraham, "Why did Sarah laugh, and say, 'Shall I indeed bear a child, now that I am old?' Is anything too wonderful for the LORD? At the set time I will return to you, in due season, and Sarah shall have a son. (Genesis 18:13–14)

Through the son of Abraham all the nations of the earth would be blessed, according to the promise God made to Abram (Abraham):

Now the LORD said to Abram: "Go from your country and your kindred and your father's house to the land that I will show you.

> I will make of you a great nation,
> and I will bless you;
> and make your name great,
> so that you will be a blessing.
> I will bless those who bless you
> And the one who curses you I will curse.
> And in you all the families of the earth
> shall be blessed." (Genesis 12:1–3)

In the Acts of the Apostles, Luke takes up the same theme in Peter's second Pentecost discourse. The promise made to Abraham is fulfilled in the mission of Jesus:

> *You are the descendants of the prophets and of the covenant that*
> *God gave to your ancestors, saying to Abraham, "And by your*
> *offspring shall all the nations of the world gain blessing"*
> *(Genesis 22:18). When God raised up his servant, he sent him*
> *first to you, to bless you by turning each of you from your wicked*
> *ways. (Acts 3:25–26)*

Symbolically expressed, the blessings brought to us by Jesus would be revealed to the apostolic community at the end of his life journey, "When the days drew near for him to be taken up, he set his face to go to Jerusalem" (Luke 9:51) where the proclamation would be made that he has risen and ascended to God (Luke 24:5–51).

"Mary Gave Birth to Her Firstborn Son" (Luke 2:7a)

We take this translation for granted. However, does Luke simply mean to tell us that Mary gave birth to *her* firstborn *(prototokon)* son? Is the emphasis on the fact that it was hers (which most translations assume), or that it was her firstborn, and not second or third? Many scriptural notes and commentaries assume one of these and explain carefully that "firstborn" is a title referring to the status of the eldest son in many ancient cultures. Evidence that the title was unrelated to whether a woman had other children comes from a first-century epitaph that refers to a young woman who died while giving birth to her firstborn son. Since she died, there was no question of her having other children.

The apologetic preoccupations of such notes are obvious. In view of the history of controversy over the perpetual virginity of Mary and the family into which Jesus was born, these apologetic concerns are not out of place. While resolving one problem, however, they may have given rise to another.

Our defensive approach to the interpretation of the text has blinded us to something we might otherwise have observed immediately. The text in Luke 2:7a is open to two quite different translations, of which the first and most obvious is not "And she gave birth to her firstborn son," but "And she gave birth to her son, the firstborn." The difference is far from minor. Exploring it will help us to appreciate the scope of Luke's statement on the Incarnation.

The first way is commonly taken for granted. Mary gave birth to a son who was her firstborn child. Given this understanding, commentaries discuss the expression "firstborn" (in Greek *prototokos*), in relation to the ancient culture in which Jesus was born, where "the firstborn" had special responsibilities and privileges in the family.

The expression indicates that this son is Mary's firstborn, and the title "firstborn" refers to his rights and obligations as the oldest son in this family. In keeping with this, we read further on in Luke 2:22–24 that

> *When the time came for their purification according to the law of Moses, they brought him up to Jerusalem to present him to the Lord (as it is written in the law of the Lord, "Every* (pan) *firstborn* (prototokon, LXX) *male* (arsen) *shall be designated as holy to the Lord," (Exodus 13:2), and they offered a sacrifice according to what is stated in the law of the Lord, "a pair of turtledoves or two young pigeons." (Leviticus 12:8)*

The expression "her firstborn" was thus a personal title, indicating nothing at all about whether Mary had other children. Even an only child would have been referred to as "firstborn." In the case of Jesus, the title would have special significance for Israelite history, highlighting Jesus' relation as firstborn to succeed to the throne of David.

The second way of understanding the expression is more theological. And there is no doubt that, at this point in the text, Luke's affirmation is mainly theological, bearing primarily on the divinity of Jesus, not on his humanity. Thus, Luke would have intended us to understand that Mary gave birth to a son who was the Firstborn, that is, the Firstborn of God. This second way of understanding the text is also suggested by the use of (firstborn) *prototokos* in the Septuagint, the Greek translation of the Bible commonly used by the early Christians in which the child was called *prototokos* in relation to the father, not the mother.

This second way also corresponds to the angel Gabriel's announcement to Mary that her son would be called Son of the Most High:

> *The angel said to her, "Do not be afraid, Mary, for you have found favor with God. And now you will conceive in your womb and bear a son, and you will name him Jesus. He will be great, and will be called the Son of the Most High, and the Lord God will give to him the throne of his ancestor David. He will reign over the house of Jacob forever, and of his kingdom there will be no end." (Luke 1:30–33)*

The Holy Spirit would come upon her and the power of the Most High overshadow *(episkiasei)*[1] her, and "therefore the child to be born will be holy; he will be called Son of God" (Luke 1:35cd). The account of the birth of Jesus adds something to the Christology of the annunciation. Mary's son, the Son of God, was God's Firstborn, just as Israel was in the Old Testament. In Exodus 4:21–23, the Pentateuch expressed the relationship:

> *And the LORD said to Moses, "Then you (Moses) shall say to Pharaoh, 'Thus says the LORD: Israel is my firstborn son*

(LXX, huios prototokos mou). I said to you, "Let my son go that he may worship me." But you refused to let him go; now I will kill your firstborn son (LXX, ton huion sou ton prototokon).' " (Exodus 4:21–23)

In Jeremiah 31:9, we see that the prophetic books understood firstborn in the same way:

*With weeping they shall come
and with consolations I will lead them back,
I will let them walk by brooks of water,
in a straight path in which they shall not stumble;
For I have become a father to Israel,
and Ephraim is my firstborn.*

As God's firstborn, Jesus' Davidic kingship would transcend Israelite history, and Jesus would reign in the kingdom of God, not over some earthly kingdom. This second understanding of the title "firstborn," also corresponds to the expression's meaning in a variety of New Testament passages.

In Romans 8:29, Paul said, in regard to Jesus, "For those whom he foreknew he also predestined to be conformed to the image *(tes eikonos)* of his Son, in order that he might be the firstborn *(auton prototokon)* within a large family *(en pollois adelphois)*." Jesus, the Son of God, was the firstborn of all those God foreknew and predestined to be conformed to the image of his Son who, as the second Adam, would restore the human race to the dignity it had in the beginning. Man and woman were created in God's image:

Then God said, "Let us make humankind (Hebrew, adam; LXX, anthropon) in our image (kat' eikonna hemeteran), according to our likeness . . . . So God created humankind in his image, in the image of God he created them; male and female he created them. (Genesis 1:26–27)

Jesus was seen as the firstborn among all those who would be reborn in Baptism, and through him share in the life and mission of Christ: "Therefore we have been buried with him by baptism into death, so that, just as Christ was raised from the dead by the glory of the Father, so we too might walk in newness of life" (Romans 6:4). A hymn in Colossians sings about the mystery of life in our Lord Jesus Christ in the same way:

He is the image of the invisible God,
the firstborn (prototokos) *of all creation* (pases ktiseos);
for in him all things in heaven and on earth were created,
things visible and invisible,
whether thrones or dominions or rulers or powers
all things have been created through him and for him.
(Colossians 1:15–16)

And again:

He is the head of the body, the church (tes ekklesias); *he is the beginning, the firstborn* (prototokos) *from the dead, so that he might come to have first place in everything. (Colossians 1:18)*

Jesus is the firstborn by reason of his relation to God the Father, and he is the firstborn as the risen Lord.

In the book of Revelation, greeting the seven churches of Asia, John invokes the grace and peace that comes from God, and the seven spirits before his throne:

Grace to you and peace from him who is and who was and who is to come, and from the seven spirits who are before his throne, and from Jesus Christ, the faithful witness, the firstborn (ho prototokos) *of the dead* (ton nekron), *and the ruler of the kings of the earth. To him who loves us and freed us from our sins by his blood . . . . (Revelation 1:4b–5)*

Again, firstborn refers to the Resurrection of Jesus and to his status with regard to all others who would enjoy risen life.

Finally in the New Testament in the letter to the Hebrews (1:5–6) in a great Christological synthesis, rich in citations from the psalms, the author asks:

> *For to which of the angels did God ever say,*
> *"You are my Son* (huios mou ei su);
> *today I have begotten you"? (Psalm 2:7bc)*

Or again,

> *"I will be his Father* (ego esomai auto eis patera),
> *and he will be my Son* (kai autos estai moi eis huion)*"?*

And again, when he brings the firstborn (ton prototokon)

> *into the world* (eis ten oikoumenen), *he says,*
> *"Let all God's angels worship him* (kai proskynesatosan auto pantes aggeloi Theou)."*

In view of these examples, all of which reflect a pervasive usage and understanding in the early Christian communities, it seems far more likely that Luke intended "firstborn" as a Christological title. "Firstborn" has connotations of the risen presence of Jesus and emphasizes how his risen life, and the life he can now share with us, came from the Father.

In all of these references, being "the firstborn" is not just a social title related to family responsibilities and privileges but a Christological title, encompassing Jesus in relation to all who are born again as Christians, to Jesus' relation to God's work of creation, to his Resurrection and to his birth, from which flow every aspect of Jesus' life and mission. By the time Luke used the title, it already had a rich history, both Israelite and Christian.

She gave birth to her son, *the firstborn of God,* the firstborn of all creatures, and firstborn from the dead! In a sense, the event seemed very ordinary. As were six billion people living on earth today, Jesus was born. In another sense, the event was quite extraordinary, as is every birth, not only for the parents to whom the child is born, but because each baby, each human being, is of inestimable worth for which there is no replacement.

In yet another sense, however, Jesus' birth was unique. The significance of every other birth comes not from what happened, that is, from the birth itself, but from the person who is born. As John put it:

> *And the Word became flesh and lived among us, and we have seen his glory, the glory as of a father's only son, full of grace and truth. No one has ever seen God. It is God the only Son,* who is close to the Father's heart *who has made him known. (John 1:14, 18)*

What happened in Jesus' birth was extraordinary, to say the least. The Word of God *(ho logos)* became flesh *(sarx)* and lived (dwelt, *eskenosen*) among us. The person who was born was equally extraordinary. Jesus was the Father's only Son. Jesus' identity as a person was inseparable from the Word becoming flesh.

As did John, Luke focused on the identity of the child. For too long, we have taken for granted that Mary "gave birth to her firstborn son" is an accurate translation of what Luke intended. The wording and the meaning appear so obvious and clear that versions in the English language are for the most part identical. A deeper familiarity with scriptural language and usage, however, should make it clear that Luke has something far more important to say. *Firstborn* is one of the great Christological titles in the New Testament.

Mary Wrapped Him in Bands of Cloth (Luke 2:7b)

Why did Luke bother to say that Mary wrapped her son in bands of cloth (swaddling cloths)?[2] Did this not happen to every child? What do bands of cloth have to do with the firstborn of the Father? Why were the bands of cloth mentioned in the Good News the angels gave to the shepherds? There is more here than meets the eye.

If Mary's son was the firstborn of God, as Luke has just assured us, the Firstborn of God was also Mary's son. And Mary wrapped him in long strips of cloth,[3] as every mother did in the ancient world. Mary wrapped bands of cloth around the Firstborn of God!

Commentaries and articles pay little or no attention to the swaddling of Jesus. This neglect goes largely unnoticed due to the many studies concerning the firstborn son, the manger, and the inn, all of which are mentioned in the verse of Luke 2:7. Those commentaries that dwell on the swaddling of Jesus focus on the precise meaning of the words or on the role of Mary. For example, in his commentary, Joseph Fitzmyer, SJ, points out that the gesture indicates Mary's maternal care, "She did for Jesus what any ancient Palestinian mother would have done for a newborn babe."[4]

This statement concerning Mary is certainly not false, but it needs to be supplemented with Christological considerations. The swaddling says something about Mary, the one who performed it. It also says something about Jesus, the one who was swaddled.

Focus on Jesus

The swaddling of Jesus sends a message about the identity and the meaning of the life of this baby.

In reading that Mary swaddled Jesus, we must not forget the preceding statement, " And she gave birth to her son, the firstborn." If "the firstborn" were but a reference to the social and cultural status of Jesus and an indication of his family rights and obligations, it would be normal to read the swaddling of Jesus as an observation concerning a cultural practice of the time.

But if *firstborn* is associated with the divine image; the one in whom all else was created; the head of the body, the Church; the one destined for primacy in all things; the faithful witness; the ruler of the kings of earth; and the one of whom the angels praised God, saying, "Glory to God in the highest heaven, and on earth peace among those whom he favors!" (2:14), then it is hard to imagine that such a wealth of associations would not have some bearing on the swaddling of Jesus.

The focus Luke has on Jesus becomes clearer from the story of the shepherds, and most especially from the message of the angel who appeared to them in glory:

> *But the angel said to them, "Do not be afraid; for see—I am bringing you good news of great joy for all the people: to you is born this day in the city of David a Savior, who is the Messiah, the Lord. This will be a sign for you: you will find a child wrapped in bands of cloth and lying in a manger." (2:10–12)*

The message of the angel is a proclamation of the Good News and a source of great joy for the shepherds and all the people. The Gospel, communicated in words, is also to be experienced in a sign: "you will find a child wrapped in bands of cloth and lying in a manger" (Luke 2:12).

In the message of the angel, swaddling is associated exclusively with Jesus, the child. No reference is made to the fact that Mary swaddled Jesus. No reference is made to Mary and Joseph at all, in spite of the fact that the two are explicitly mentioned a little later when the shepherds go to Bethlehem as the angel had directed: "So they went with haste and found Mary and Joseph, and the child lying in the manger" (2:16).

To understand the significance of the terms firstborn and swaddling, we will compare the narratives of the birth of Jesus with that of John the Baptist. Reading the prologue of Luke we see that the annunciation and birth story of Jesus parallels that of John. This literary parallel draws attention to the historical and religious links between their respective missions. Departures from the parallel presentations are significant. They point to the differences between the two and highlight the way the life and mission of Jesus transcends that of John.

Examining the accounts of the two births, we find that in both cases Luke states that the time for the mother to give birth had been fulfilled. After this introductory statement, we are told, again in both cases, that the mother gave birth to a son. Up to this point, the parallel presentation is maintained. However, while nothing further is said about the birth of John, the story of Jesus continues with the circumcision and purification.

In the case of John, there is no reference to his being the firstborn, a strange omission after Luke's emphasis on the childlessness of his parents, their advanced years, and the sterility of Elizabeth (Luke 1:7, 18, 36). Nor is there any reference to the swaddling of John by his mother. By not including such statements in the first of the two birth accounts, Luke draws attention to their special significance in the story of Jesus. This would not have been necessary, and even pointless, if references to the firstborn and his being swaddled had been simple cultural observations.

A Mortal Human Being

Everything suggests that the swaddling of Jesus, the firstborn, is a significant Christological statement in Luke. To uncover its significance, we need some assistance from the Old Testament. Fitzmyer says in his commentary that some of the details in Luke 2:7 are important "not only because they will become part of the sign given to the shepherds but because of their symbolic character. They are like allusions in a tone poem to Old Testament motifs."[5]

References to swaddling, though, are almost as rare in the Old Testament as in the New Testament. The only examples in the New Testament are Galatians 3:26–29 and the two references Luke makes in the prologue. In the Old Testament, we have three texts: Job 38:8–9, Ezekiel 16:4–5, and Wisdom 7:4.

In Job, the reference to swaddling comes in the speech the Lord makes in chapter 38: "Then the LORD answered Job out of the whirlwind" (verse 1). Job already has been reminded of his creaturely status:

> *Where were you when I laid the foundation of the earth?*
> *(Job 38:4)*

> *Or who shut in the sea with doors*
> *when it burst out from the womb?—*
> *when I made the clouds its garment,*
> *and thick darkness its swaddling band.*
> *(Job 38:8–9)*

The birth and swaddling of the sea help us to appreciate the evocative power of swaddling bands.

In the prophecy of Ezekiel, a reference to swaddling and swaddling cloths forms part of the devastating description the Lord God makes of the origins of Jerusalem when the city became a faithless spouse.

> *As for your birth, on the day you were born your navel cord was*
> *not cut, nor were you washed with water to cleanse you, nor*
> *rubbed with salt, nor wrapped in cloth. No eye pitied you to do*
> *any of these things for you out of compassion for you; but you*
> *were thrown out in the open field, for you were abhorrent on the*
> *day you were born.*

The nakedness of Jerusalem at birth helps us to appreciate the ignominy of being without swaddling cloths.

Sensitized to a great Old Testament metaphor, we now turn to the poetic discourse attributed to Solomon in Wisdom 7:1–6. On the lips of Solomon, being wrapped in swaddling cloths joins the experience of human birth in a statement about the mortality and destiny of every human being.

> *I also am mortal, like everyone else,*
> *a descendant of the first-formed child of earth;*
> *and in the womb of a mother I was molded into flesh,*
> *within the period of ten months, compacted with blood,*
> *from the seed of a man and the pleasure of marriage.*
> *And when I was born, I began to breathe the common air,*
> *and fell upon the kindred earth;*
> *my first sound was a cry, as is true of all.*
> *I was nursed with care in swaddling cloths*
> *For no king has had a different beginning of existence;*
> *there is for all one entrance into life, and one way out.*

The passage begins and ends with the theme of mortality, the lot of everyone who descends from Adam. Solomon, king that he was, realized that the simple origin shared by all—whether king or pauper—announced the simple end of life in which all would share. The swaddling cloths are the climactic symbol expressing this.

In Galatians, Paul does not speak in any detail of Baptism as he does in Romans 6:1–11. He supposes that his audience knows what he means because they have been baptized. Paul views Baptism as an act of being clothed in Christ. It is the moment when Christ, like a garment, envelops the believer.

> *For in Christ Jesus you are all children of God through faith.*
> *As many of you as were baptized into Christ have clothed*
> *yourselves with Christ. There is no longer Jew or Greek, there*

*is no longer slave or free, there is no longer male and female; for
all of you are one in Christ Jesus. And if you belong to Christ,
then you are Abraham's offspring, heirs according to the promise.
(Galatians 3:26–29)*

Although Paul does not employ the word "garment," he
describes the righteousness conferred upon believers. He writes,
"He is the source of your life in Christ Jesus, who became for us
wisdom from God, and righteousness and sanctification and
redemption" (1 Corinthians 1:30).

On the concept of being clothed with righteousness and salvation, Isaiah had elaborated:

> *I will greatly rejoice in the Lord,*
> *my whole being shall exult in my God;*
> *for he has clothed me* (enedyse gar me) *with the garments*
> *(LXX,* himation*) of salvation* (soteriou),
> *he has covered me with the robe of righteousness*
> (kai chitona euphrosynes, *and the garment of joy),*
> *as a bridegroom decks himself with a garland*
> (perietheke moi mitran, *he has put a mitre on me),*
> *and as a bride adorns herself with her jewels*
> (katekosmese me kosmo, *adorned me*
> *with ornaments). (Isaiah 61:10)*

The prologue emphasizes that Jesus was the firstborn, the Son
of God, true; but it also points to the mortality of Jesus and the bru-
tal death he would endure:

> *Then Simeon blessed them and said to his mother Mary, "This
> child is destined for the falling and the rising of many in Israel,
> and to be a sign that will be opposed so that the inner thoughts
> of many will be revealed—and a sword will pierce your own
> soul too." (Luke 2:34–35)*

As the firstborn from the dead, Jesus had to be mortal. The expression firstborn implied the Resurrection of Jesus and pointed to his rebirth into the heavenly kingdom of the Father. The description "wrapped him in bands of cloth" implied mortality and pointed to the death he would experience in the city of David. Jesus was wrapped in swaddling cloths and laid in a manger just as he would one day be wrapped in a linen cloth and laid in a tomb:

> Now there was a good and righteous man named Joseph, who, though a member of the council, had not agreed to their plan and action. He came from the Jewish town of Arimathea, and he was waiting expectantly for the kingdom of God. This man went to Pilate and asked for the body of Jesus. Then he took it down, wrapped it in a linen cloth (sindoni, linen cloth [made of flax] of good, fine quality for burial), and laid it in a rock-hewn tomb where no one had ever been laid. (Luke 23:50–53)

Mary Laid Him in a Manger (Luke 2:7c)

The Lukan account of the birth of Jesus is a synthesis of the Gospel message. The Christmas season invites us to reexamine our image of the manger. The manger is significant enough to be mentioned several times and to be the sign whereby the shepherds would recognize their Savior and Messiah. We will see that it is presented as a powerful expression of the nourishing presence of Jesus for all who join the shepherds at the table of the manger.

"And she (Mary) laid him *(aneklinen auton)* in a manger *(en phatne,* a feeding trough)" (Luke 2:7). We have repeated these words so often that they have lost much of their power. It no longer strikes us as unusual that Mary would have placed her newborn in a manger. Laying Jesus in a manger, however, should evoke the memory of the Septuagint version of Isaiah 1:3: "The ox knows its owner, and the donkey its master's crib *(ten phatnen,* manger); but Israel does not know, my people do not understand."

For Luke, however, placing Jesus in a manger was an extraordinary event, a sign from heaven, an eloquent expression of the personal identity and mission of Jesus, and a symbolic synthesis of the Gospel. Luke refers to the manger three times. It first appears in the one-sentence narrative of Jesus' birth:

> *And she gave birth to her firstborn son*
> *and wrapped him in bands of cloth,*
> and laid him in a manger,
> *because there was no place for them in the inn.* (2:7)

It next appears in the story of the shepherds, where it is part of the angel's proclamation of the Good News:

> *But the angel said to them, "Do not be afraid; for see—I am*
> *bringing you good news of great joy for all the people; to you is*
> *born this day in the city of David a Savior, who is the Messiah,*
> *the Lord. This will be a sign for you: you will find a child*
> *wrapped in bands of cloth* and lying in a manger." (2:10–12)

Finally, it appears in the account of the shepherds' visit to Bethlehem:

> *When the angels had left them and gone into heaven, the*
> *shepherds said to one another, "Let us go now to Bethlehem*
> *and see this thing that has taken place, which the Lord*
> *has made known to us." So they went with haste and found*
> *Mary and Joseph,* and the child lying in the manger
> (kai to brephos [the baby, the infant] keimenon en
> te phatne). *When they saw this, they made known what had*
> *been told them about this child; and all who heard it were*
> *amazed at what the shepherds told them.* (2:15–18)

We have already considered other important motifs in Luke's account. The city of David is mentioned in the introduction as well as in the message the angels bring to the shepherds. The swaddling cloths are an important symbol in the statement of the birth of Jesus (2:7), and they, too, are mentioned twice. However, only the manger figures three times in every part of the narrative (2:7c, 12c, 16b). Literarily, it is the most important motif in the Lukan account of the birth of Jesus.

The Manger (he phatne)

After swaddling the Firstborn of God, who was her son, human and mortal just like us, Mary laid him in a manger.[6] A manger is a feeding trough for animals. In ancient Palestine, where wood was scarce and stone plentiful, mangers were usually made of stone, either free-standing or hewn from the bedrock. Jesus' manger could have been in an open courtyard, corral, a kind of stable, or in a cave somewhere in Bethlehem. Luke does not say.

Why a manger? Nothing indicated so far gives grounds for laying Jesus in a manger. Continuing, Luke gives a reason: "because there was no place for them *in the inn (en to katalymati)*" (Luke 2:7d). With no room in the inn, Mary and Joseph had to seek shelter elsewhere. But wherever that was, surely there would have been at least a mat on which to sleep. Why did Mary not lay Jesus on a mat? If it were possible to find swaddling cloths, it should have been just as easy to obtain a mat.

To discover the significance of the manger as a literary and theological motif, we must first explore the image and what it calls to mind. The Greek word for manger is *phatne,* a term which can also refer to a stall or any kind of feeding place for animals, including an enclosure open to the sky. In Luke 13:15–16, the only other instance where *phatne* is used in the New Testament, it does not have the narrower meaning of manger but the broader one of stall or enclosure, which, of course, would normally have included a manger.

*But the Lord answered him (the leader of the synagogue) and
said, "You hypocrites! Does not each of you on the Sabbath
untie his ox or his donkey from the manger* (apo tes phatnes),
*and lead it away to give it water? And ought not this woman,
a daughter of Abraham whom Satan bound for eighteen long
years be set free* (edei lythenai) *from this bondage on the
sabbath day."*

The key to the meaning of *phatne* in this rhetorical question is
the verb *lyo,* which means to loose, untie, release, or set free. One
does not release animals from a manger, but from some kind of
restricting space or structure that prevents the animals from going
to the water by themselves.

The use of *phatne* in Luke 13:15 in the broader sense of stall
raises the question concerning its use in 2:7c, 12c, and 16b. In these
three related cases, however, the verbs point toward the narrower
sense of manger, a simple trough that holds feed for domestic animals and from which they feed. The act of laying the child in a
phatne calls for something more specific than a stall. Had there been
room in the inn, we cannot imagine that Luke would have said that
Mary laid him in the inn. The place indicated would have been too
general for the verb associated with it. The same applies to stall.

Further, in Luke 2:16, the shepherds find Mary and Joseph
and the child, who alone was said to be in the manger. If Luke had
had the broader meaning of stall in mind, it would seem he would
have said the shepherds found Mary and Joseph and the child in
the *phatne.* Yet only the child was in the *phatne.* The most probable
meaning of *phatne* in Luke 2:1–20 is thus "manger," the term we
have been using all along and which we find in our English translations. Nothing is said of the place where the manger was. We are
not told whether it was in a stable or some other kind of enclosure.

The image Luke raises before us is that of the manger itself.
It should draw all of our attention. Other considerations of place

are distractions that prevent our discovering the meaning of the manger motif in Luke.

A good way to focus our imagination and sharpen our perception is to retranslate Luke 2:7 as the following: "Mary gave birth to her son, the Firstborn of God, and wrapped him in bands of cloth, and laid him in a feeding trough, because there was no place for them in the inn." When we think of the feeding trough in which Mary places Jesus, we should also take care to imagine something made of stone. Stone was the common substance in the Holy Land, and the art of cutting and trimming it was highly developed. Wood, which was rare, would have been far too expensive to use for an ordinary feeding-trough.

The Manger as Sign (to semeion)

The manger is a striking image, precisely because it is so unlikely. There is no question about its meaningfulness. The image was an important part of the proclamation of the Good News to the shepherds: "This (touto) will be a sign (to semeion) for you (hymin): you will find a child wrapped in bands of cloth and lying in a manger" (Luke 2:12).

The child swaddled and lying in a manger is not a proof of the authenticity of the good news but an eloquent expression of its meaning. Later, when the shepherds saw the infant lying in a manger, they proclaimed the message that was announced to them. The child was indeed a Savior born to them, one who was Messiah, the Lord (2:11), whose Good News would bring great joy to all people.

The sign is revelatory, an integral part of the Gospel that was proclaimed in word by the angel and a visible sign by the child lying in the manger. This is clear from the reaction of the shepherds to the sign. We are not told that they believed what the angel said. We are told that they understood what the angel told them.

At the Table of the Manger

For us as well as the shepherds, the laying of Jesus in a feeding trough is a sign, a symbolic expression of the Good News that a Savior, who is Christ and Lord, has come for all people. We are now in a position to grasp the intent when Luke writes that Mary laid her son, the firstborn of God, in a manger because there was no place for them in the inn.

The city of David, Bethlehem, did not welcome and extend hospitality to the heir of David, the firstborn of God. At the end of the Gospel according to Luke, Jesus is rejected in Jerusalem. However, the account of the Last Supper (22:14–38) shows how this rejection became the occasion for Jesus' total gift of himself as nourishment. In doing so, he transformed what would have been a Passion suffered at the hands of others into an action consciously undertaken on behalf of all.

The relationship of the manger to the titles of Savior, Messiah, and Lord is now clear. It is by giving his life in nourishment that Jesus saves us and is Savior. At the end of Acts, the words of Paul to all aboard the ship during a storm dramatically present the relationship between the breaking of bread and salvation in dramatic terms:

> *Just before daybreak, Paul urged all of them to take* (metalabein)
> *some food* (trophes), *saying, "Today is the fourteenth day*
> *that you have been in suspense and remaining without food*
> (asitoi), *having eaten nothing. Therefore I urge you to take*
> (metalabein) *some food* (trophes), *for it will help you survive;*
> *for none of you will lose a hair from your heads." After he had*
> *said this, he took* (labon) *bread* (arton); *and giving thanks*
> (eucharistesen) *to God in the presence of all, he broke* (klasas)
> *it and began to eat* (esthiein). *(Acts 27:33–35)*

It is also by offering his life as nourishment, by drinking the cup according to the will of his Father, by accepting to die for us, that Jesus became Christ (Messiah) and Lord. "Therefore let the entire house of Israel know with certainty that God has made him both Lord and Messiah (Christ), this Jesus whom you crucified" (Acts 2:36).

Luke writes in the Acts of the Apostles: "they devoted themselves to the apostles' teaching and fellowship *(te koinonia)*, to the breaking of bread *(te klasei tou artou)* and the prayers. Day by day, as they spent much time together in the temple, they broke bread at home *(klontes te kat' oikon arton)* and ate their food *(metelambanon trophes)* with glad and generous hearts"[7] (Acts 2:42, 47).

No Room for Them in the Inn

Had Luke not mentioned the inn at Bethlehem, we would know nothing about it. We certainly would not know that it figured in the events of the birth of Jesus and that there was no room there for Joseph and his young wife Mary, who was about to give birth. If Matthew, who also spoke of the birth of Jesus in Bethlehem (Matthew 2:1–12), knew of such an incident, he did not record it.

For Luke, however, it was important to mention the inn and that there was no place there for Mary and Joseph at the time of the birth. The statement concludes the narrative of the birth of Jesus: "And she gave birth to her firstborn son and wrapped him in bands of cloth, and laid him in a manger, because *(dioti)* there was no place for them *(ouk en autois topos)* in the inn *(en to katalymati)*" (2:7).

Reflection on the meaning of the inn usually begins with the meaning of the word Luke employed in Greek, *katalyma,* and the way he employed it. In the Septuagint, the word *katalyma,* which we normally translate in English as "inn" refers to a place of hospitality for people on a journey. This could be something akin to an inn, of course, and in this case it might well have resembled one of the caravanserais we have come to know from more recent history. But it could also be any other place where a traveler was received for the night. It could even be a home. To translate *katalyma* as an inn is consequently too restrictive unless the context calls for it.

Luke uses *katalyma* in a more general sense. In addition to its usage in 2:7d, the noun appears in the instructions Jesus gave for preparing the Passover:

> *So Jesus sent Peter and John, saying, "Go and prepare the*
> *Passover meal for us that we may eat it." They asked him,*
> *"Where do you want us to make preparations for it?" "Listen,"*
> *he said to them, "when you have entered the city, a man carrying*
> *a jar of water will meet you; follow him into the house he*
> *enters and say to the owner of the house, 'The teacher asks you,*
> *"Where is the guest room* (to katalyma), *where I may eat*
> *the Passover with my disciples?" ' He will show you a large room*
> (anagaion mega) *upstairs, already furnished. Make preparations*
> *for us there." (Luke 22:8–12)*

In this case, the *katalyma* is not an inn for lodging overnight but an upstairs room suitable for dining. The verb *katalyo*, which is related to the noun *katalyma*, also appears twice in Luke. In the story of the feeding of the five thousand, it reads:

> *The day was drawing to a close, and the twelve came to him*
> *and said, "Send the crowd away, so that they may go into the*
> *surrounding villages and countryside, to lodge* (katalysosin)
> *and get provisions; for we are here in a deserted place."[8] (9:12)*

In the story of Zacchaeus, it expresses the intention of Jesus to stay at the rich tax collector's home:

> *So [Zacchaeus] ran ahead and climbed a sycamore tree to see*
> *him, because he was going to pass that way. When Jesus came to*
> *the place he looked up and said to him, "Zacchaeus, hurry and*
> *come down; for I must stay at your house today." So he hurried*
> *down and was happy to welcome him. All who saw it began*

to grumble and said, "He has gone to be the guest (katalysai)[9] *of one who is a sinner." (19:4–7)*

Thus, though the Greek word *katalyma* can mean an inn, Luke, in the story of Jesus' birth, does not use it in this restricted sense. Where Luke clearly has an inn in mind, as in the story of the Good Samaritan, he uses a different word:

Jesus replied:

> *But a Samaritan while traveling came near him; and when he saw him, he was moved with pity. He went to him and bandaged his wounds, having poured oil and wine on them. Then he put him on his own animal, brought him to an inn (eis pandocheion), and took care of him. The next day he took out two denarii (dyo denaria, two Roman silver coins equivalent to the two days' wage of a common laborer), gave them to the innkeeper (to pandochei), and said, "Take care of him; and when I come back, I will repay you whatever more you spend." (10:30–35)*

Luke did not use the word *katalyma* here, but *pandocheion*, a place run by an innkeeper *(pandocheus)* and where a traveler pays for lodging. Luke's "inn," or guest facility of some kind, is thus clearly associated with two important themes of Luke's account, that of the journey[10] and that of hospitality. The story of the birth of Jesus is part of a journey from Nazareth to Bethlehem and Jerusalem (and back to Nazareth).

The prologue alone includes two other journeys from Nazareth, that of Mary to the home of Zechariah in the hill country of Judah (1:39–56) and that of Jesus and his parents to Jerusalem when Jesus was twelve years old (2:41–51).

The most important journey in Luke is that of Jesus and his disciples from Galilee to Jerusalem (9:51—24:53): "When the days drew near for him to be taken up, he set his face to go to Jerusalem."

There we see that Luke uses the geographical setting of a journey as a literary device to speak of the entire life of Jesus as a journey to God his Father. Geographically, the journey ends when Jesus arrives in Jerusalem, but thematically it extends to the Ascension. This journey, which focuses on Jesus' ultimate destiny, situates the life and teaching of Jesus in relation to their fulfillment in the company of the Father.

Hospitality and Rejection

Along the journey, which is personal as well as missionary, Jesus receives hospitality on numerous occasions. There is, for example, the hospitality in the home of Martha, where Martha learns that true service *(diakonia)* consists in attention to the guest and listening attentively to the word of the Lord (Luke 10:38–42). The Lord's Prayer follows: "He (Jesus) said to them (disciples), 'When you pray, say: Father, hallowed be your name. Your kingdom come. Give us *(didou hemin)* each day *(kath' hemeran)* our daily *(hemon ton epiousion)* bread (ton arton)'" (11:2–3).[11]

There is the hospitality given him by a leading Pharisee (14:1–24) as well as that joyfully extended by Zacchaeus (19:1-10). The Last Supper that Jesus offered us in Jerusalem, in the *katalyma,* the spacious upstairs room, is part of that journey.

On the journey, there are also those who refuse to welcome Jesus. At the very start of his long journey to Jerusalem there were the Samaritans (9:52), and toward its end one of his disciples conspired with the chief priests and the scribes to transform the Passover hospitality *(katalyma)* in Jerusalem into a place of rejection and betrayal (22:1–5, 21–23). Some found a place for him and his disciples in the *katalyma* at Jerusalem, but for others there was none, just as there had been no place for them in the *katalyma* at Bethlehem (2:7).

The statement in 2:7 that there was no place for them in the *katalyma,* however, does not explicitly say that Jesus was rejected there. The expression "there was no place for them" (2:7d) is neutral. It is open to meaning rejection as well as to another interpretation closely associated with the missionary aspect of the journey to God. When someone says to Jesus, "I will follow you wherever you go" (9:57), Jesus responds, "Foxes have holes, and birds of the air have nests; but the Son of Man has nowhere to lay his head" (9:58).

The journey's missionary vision is the coming of the reign of God. Those who join Jesus and dedicate their lives for the establishment of the kingdom cannot settle in any particular place. The kingdom is universal. It includes all peoples and nations and embraces the human race. It also transcends every earthly manifestation. That is why the Son of Man, *the human being,* has no place to lay his head.

The statement that there was no place for them in the *katalyma* consequently says something about the rejection of Jesus, but it also says something about the purpose of his life. Jesus must announce the Good News of the reign of God to other villages, towns, and cities because that is why he was sent (4:43). Ultimately, he must be with his Father in his heavenly home, the definitive *katalyma* or place of hospitality at the end of his life journey (2:49; 24:50–53).

Reflection on Mary's Son, the Firstborn of God

Our reflections have left philological, physical, and architectural considerations far behind. These were not unimportant, for they allowed us to enter the literary world of Luke. Of far greater significance is the message that Luke wants us to hear. That there was no room in the *katalyma* announced several themes that lie at the heart of Lukan theology. And one thing we know from the immediate context about the katalyma is that it referred to the hospitality that Bethlehem provided travelers and Jesus in particular.

Bethlehem already has figured significantly in Luke 2:4–5. Luke presents it as the city of David. The *katalyma* that Jesus should have found as a descendant of David in the city of David was not afforded him. Luke's readers would have associated the lack of hospitality that Jesus received at the beginning of his life in Bethlehem as prefiguring the greater rejection that he would suffer in Jerusalem. By calling Bethlehem the city of David, Luke evokes the end of the life journey of Jesus in Jerusalem, the place that welcomed him only to finally reject him, and from which he would journey on to the home of his Father.

There was no place for them in the hospitality of the city of David. The city of David did not welcome the one whom God had raised as a horn of saving strength in the house of David his servant (1:69). There was no place in the hospitality of the city of David for the one to whom God would give the throne of David his father (1:32). For him there was only the blindness and rejection of Bethlehem. The passage also evokes the mission and purpose of Jesus. The Son of Man was not to lay his head on an earthly throne of David. His kingdom was not of this world.

> The angel (Gabriel) said to her (Mary) "He will be great, and will be called the Son of the Most High, and the Lord God will give to him the throne of his ancestor David. He will reign over the house of Jacob forever, and of his kingdom there will be no end." (Luke 1:30, 32–33)

The fact that there was no place in Bethlehem's hospitality is given as the reason why Mary laid the firstborn in a manger. More is found in the manger than a mere statement of fact.

1. "In the phrase 'the power of the Most High will overshadow you,' the word 'overshadow' *(episkiakei)* evokes the presence of God in the form of a cloud upon the Israelite sanctuary or the tabernacle during the Israelite Exodus (Exodus 40:34–40)," E. LaVerdiere, *The Annunciation to Mary: A Story of Faith, Luke 1:26–38* (Chicago: Liturgy Training Publications, 2004), 128.

2. Luke Timothy Johnson wrote: "*wrapped him in cloth strips:* Strips or bands of cloths were wrapped around a newborn to keep the limbs straight by means of restraint," *The Gospel of Luke* (Sacra Pagina 3), (Collegeville, Minnesota: The Liturgical Press, 1991), 50, in note of Luke 2:7.

3. J. A. Fitzmyer wrote: "Lit. swaddled him," because the Greek verb *sparganoun* is derived from the noun *sparganon,* "cloth band," *The Gospel According to Luke I–IX* (The Anchor Bible 28), (Garden City, New York: Doubleday and Company, Inc., 1981), 408, note of Luke 2:7 wrapped him in cloth bands.

4. Ibid.

5. Op. Cit., 394.

6. Alfred Plummer, DD, *A Critical and Exegetical Commentary on the Gospel According to Saint Luke,* The International Critical Commentary (Edinburgh: T. and T. Clark, 1964), 51–52, en phatne, note 2:7, "Justin (Try. Lxxviii.) and some of the apocryphal gospels say that it was in a cave, which is not improbable."

7. E. LaVerdiere, *The Breaking of the Bread,* ibid., 75–102.

8. For an explanation of the significance of "deserted," refer to E. LaVerdiere, *Dining in the Kingdom of God,* 65–66.

9. Ibid., 113–117.

10. E. LaVerdiere, *Luke,* New Testament 5 (Collegeville, Minnesota: The Liturgical Press, 1980, 1990), 138–143, C. *The Journey: Jesus and the Destiny of the Church (Luke 9:51, 24:53).*

The Shepherds and the Angels

In that region there were shepherds living
in the fields, keeping watch over their flock by night.
Then an angel of the Lord stood before them,
and the glory of the Lord shone around them,
and they were terrified. But the angel said to them,
"Do not be afraid; for see—I am bringing you good news
of great joy for all the people: to you is born this day in
the city of David a Savior, who is the Messiah (Christ),
the Lord. This will be a sign for you: you will find a child
wrapped in bands of cloth and lying in a manger."
And suddenly there was with the angel a multitude
of the heavenly host, praising God and saying,
"Glory to God in the highest heaven,
and on earth peace among those
whom he favors!" (Luke 2:8–14)

Why Shepherds?

In Luke 2:8–14, angels introduce the shepherds in the account that contains their proclamation of the birth of Jesus, followed by the song of the angels. The obvious question is: "Why should angels announce Jesus' birth only to shepherds?" What is the significance of having shepherds be first to hear the Gospel? This was nothing accidental. The announcement came to them from heaven, just as did the annunciation of the conception of Jesus (1:26–38) and, before that the annunciation of the conception of John the Baptist (1:5–25).

The shepherds also will be the first to respond to the Gospel. As with the disciples of John the Baptist (see 7:18–23), they do not only hear the Gospel. They see its concrete expression in life and history. They go to Bethlehem and see the event that was announced to them. Upon seeing, they understand what the angel made known to them.

The shepherds, as we will see, are also the first to proclaim the Gospel, and all who heard them were astonished at what they were told. The Good News was not for them alone.

Finally, the shepherds, the first to hear, experience, and proclaim the Gospel, glorify and praise God for everything they had seen and heard in accord with what the angel told them.

Their response echoes that of the heavenly host (2:13–14) and anticipates that of those who would later hear Jesus (4:15), be healed by him (4:25; 13:13; 17:15), or witness his healing and life-giving power at work (4:26; 7:16; 18:43). Their response was the response of disciples (19:37) or that of a centurion to the death of Jesus on the cross (23:47). It was the response of the early Christian community (Acts 2:47).

From this brief review of the role of the shepherds, it becomes clear that Luke has the disciples and the early Christian community in mind when he speaks of the shepherds. This raises an obvious question about their flock. Somehow, it must be related to the life of the universal Church. And it is.

Jesus addresses his disciples as a "little flock" when he tells them not to fear:

Do not be afraid, little flock (to micron poimnion),[1] *for it is your Father's good pleasure to give you the kingdom. Sell your possessions, and give alms. Make purses for yourselves that do*

not wear out, an unfailing treasure in heaven, where no thief
comes near and no moth destroys. For where your treasure is,
there your heart will be also. (12:32–34)

In the Gospel according to Luke, the evangelist refers to the community of disciples as a "little flock" to whom the Father was pleased to give the kingdom. In the Acts of the Apostles, Paul addresses the elders (*hoi presbyteroi,* the presbyters) in Ephesus (20:18–35) as overseers of the flock, an image for the church in its various communities:

> *"Keep watch over yourselves and over all the flock* (panti
> to poimnio), *of which the Holy Spirit has made you overseers*
> (episkopous, bishops), *to shepherd* (poimainein) *the church*
> *of God that he obtained with the blood of his own Son. I know*
> *that after I have gone, savage wolves* (lykoi) *will come in among*
> *you, not sparing* (me pheidomenoi) *the flock* (tou poimniou)."
> *(Acts 20:28–29)*

These passages allow us to further refine our understanding of the place of shepherds in the infancy narrative. The story of the shepherds standing watch over their flock evokes the Church and its elders, the presbyters, those who were leading the Church in the time of Luke. The story of the shepherds is the story of the Church in miniature.

The Task of Shepherds (Luke 2:8)

The sign of the manger and the gospel it proclaimed was given to shepherds keeping watch over their flock. Having examined the manger image and the purpose of the sign, we must also take a closer look at the shepherds, and how their tasks are described in the scriptures.

Tending the flocks was responsible work, especially during the rains in Palestine from November to April. In view of the threat of wild beasts and robbers it was dangerous, as evidenced in this passage from 1 Samuel 17:34–37:

> But David said to Saul, "Your servant used to keep sheep for his father; and whenever a lion or a bear came, and took a lamb from the flock. I went after it and struck it down, rescuing the lamb from its mouth; and if it turned against me, I would catch it by the jaw, strike it down, and kill it. Your servant has killed both lions and bears; and this uncircumcised Philistine (robber) shall be like one of them, since he has defied the armies of the living God." David said, "The LORD, who saved me from the paw of the lion and from the paw of the bear, will save me from the hand of this Philistine (robber)."

The association of the shepherd David from Bethlehem who was a great warrior and one of Israel's most distinguished kings is proof that God can use the lowly of this world as key players in salvation history.

The shepherd imagery is prominent in the New Testament. Luke lists three parables that Jesus told the Pharisees and scribes who were accusing him of always eating and drinking with tax collectors and sinners: the lost sheep (15:4–7), the lost coin (15:8–10), and the lost (prodigal) son (15:11–32). We note in the first parable that sometimes the owner of the sheep or his sons did the work of shepherding:

> Which one of you, having a hundred sheep (probata) and losing one (hen) of them, does not leave the ninety-nine in the wilderness and go after the one that is lost (epi to apololos) until he finds it? When he has found it, he lays it on his shoulders and rejoices. And when he comes home, he calls together his friends and neighbors, saying to them, "Rejoice with me, for I have found

my sheep (to probaton mou) *that was lost* (to apololos)."
Just so, I tell you, there will be more joy in heaven over one
sinner who repents than over ninety-nine righteous persons who
need no repentance.

Sometimes, however, the shepherds were hired hands who only too often did not justify the confidence placed in them, according to John 10:12–13:

Jesus said to them (the Pharisees), "The hired hand who
is not the shepherd and does not own the sheep, sees the wolf
coming and leaves the sheep and runs away—and the wolf
snatches them and scatters them. The hired hand runs away
because a hired hand does not care for the sheep."

The true shepherd protects the sheep by lying across the gate of the stone corral at night. So again Jesus said to them, "Very truly, I tell you, I am *(ego eimi)* the gate *(he thyra)* for the sheep" (John 10:7). In the Gospel according to John, Jesus says, "I am *(ego eimi)* the good shepherd *(ho poimen ho kalos)*. The good shepherd lays down his life for the sheep" (John 10:11). As we have already seen, the child lying in a manger is already a sign of the gift of life that Jesus will make so that we might live. This dominant image will give flesh to the titles that the angel will give to Jesus in his announcement to the shepherds.

Shepherd imagery was carried over and applied to the Church as well. We see that, from the earliest days, the leaders of the Church were likened to shepherds. Thus, Saint Paul speaks to the presbyters of the church at Ephesus: "Keep watch over yourselves and over all the flock *(panti to poimnio)*, of which the Holy Spirit has made you overseers *(episkopous)*, to shepherd *(poimainein)* the church of God that he obtained with the blood of his own Son" (Acts 20:28).[2]

The role Peter held in the Church is described as that of a shepherd appointed by the risen Lord. His work would encompass the whole Church.

When they had finished breakfast, Jesus said to Simon Peter, "Simon son of John, do you love (agapas) me more than these (pleon touton)?" He said to him, "Yes, Lord; you know that I love (philo) you." Jesus said to him, "Feed (Boske) my lambs (ta arnia mou)." A second time he said to him, "Simon son of John, do you love (agapas) me?" He said to him, "Yes, Lord; you know that I love (philo) you." Jesus said to him, "Tend (poimaine) my sheep (ta probate mou)." He said to him the third time, "Simon son of John, do you love (phileis) me?" Peter felt hurt because he said to him the third time, "Do you love (phileis) me?" And he said to him, "Lord you know everything; you know that I love (philo) you." Jesus said to him, "Feed (boske) my sheep (ta probate)." (John 21:15–17)

Church leaders prove themselves to be good shepherds when they fulfill their mission with commitment to the flock. According to 1 Peter 5:1–4:

I exhort the elders among you to tend (poimanate) the flock (to poimnion)[3] of God that is in your charge, exercising the oversight, not under compulsion but willingly, as God would have you do it—not for sordid gain but eagerly. Do not lord it over those in your charge, but be examples to the flock (tou poimniou). And when the chief shepherd (archipoimenos)[4] appears, you will win the crown of glory that never fades away.

In the writings of Bishop Ignatius of Antioch at the beginning of the second century, Church leaders continued to be portrayed as "shepherds." To the Romans, Ignatius writes, "Remember in your prayers the Church in Syria, which now has God for its shepherd, instead of me. Jesus Christ alone will oversee it . . . ."[5]

In a letter to the Philadelphians 2:1, Ignatius says, "Therefore as children of the light of truth flee from division and wrong doctrine. And follow as sheep where the shepherd is."[6]

The shepherds in the infancy narrative are in this tradition at the birth of Jesus in the manger. They foreshadow what will be the ongoing role of leaders in the Church. As distinct from the figurative sayings about shepherds in Luke 15:3–7 and John 10:7–13, we find real shepherds in the account Luke gives of the Nativity. The discussion has been leading us to the way in which shepherds are presented in the Christmas story. This is an important issue, since the answer helps to determine our assessment of the story of the birth of Jesus.

An Angel of the Lord (Luke 2:9)

"Then an angel of the Lord stood before them, and the glory of the Lord shone around them and they were terrified" (2:9). Announcement stories in the scriptures all have a similar pattern. There is the appearance of an angel of the Lord, fear on the part of the one(s) receiving the message, an injunction not to be afraid, the message itself, an objection on the part of one receiving the message regarding its fulfillment, and the giving of some sign that the message is authentic. In this case there is no objection (Mary's "How can this be . . . ?" [1:34] is but one such example).

The angel, of course, represents God. And so the glory of the Lord would naturally shine about him. The glory of the Lord in heavenly brightness is a sign of the presence of God, according to Exodus 16:6–7, 10:

> So Moses and Aaron said to all the Israelites, "In the evening
> you shall know that it was the Lord who brought you out
> of the land of Egypt, and in the morning you shall see the glory
> (Hebrew, kabod; LXX, ten doxan) of the Lord (Kyriou)
> because he has heard your complaining against the LORD."

And as Aaron spoke to the whole congregation of the Israelites, they looked toward the wilderness, and the glory of the LORD appeared in the cloud.

This heavenly glory would be seen in the transfiguration of Jesus. While he was in communion with God, his face shone, and his clothes became dazzling white, according to Luke 9:30–32:

Suddenly they saw two men, Moses and Elijah, talking to him. They appeared (ophthentes) *in glory* (en doxe) *and were speaking of his departure* (ten exodon autou), *which he was about to accomplish at Jerusalem. Now Peter and his companions (John and James) were weighed down with sleep; but since they had stayed awake, they saw his glory* (ten doxan autou) *and the two men who stood with him.*

This was the glory referred to when the risen Christ appeared on the road to Emmaus (24:13–35). Jesus would enter definitively into the glory of God only after his Resurrection.

Then he (the risen Jesus) said to them (Clopas and the other individual), "Oh, how foolish you are, and how slow of heart to believe all that the prophets have declared! Was it not necessary that the Messiah (the Christ) should suffer these things and then enter into his glory?" (24:25–26)

The shepherds in the region of Bethlehem were struck with great fear at the appearance of the glory of the Lord. Literally, "they feared *(ephobethesan)* a great fear *(phobon megan)*" (2:9c). This is the natural fear and sense of awe that results from recognizing the great distance that separates us from the perfection of God, the complete otherness of God. The transcendence of God is manifested at times in storms and other extraordinary manifestations of nature. We still capture some sense of this in the liturgy, where we echo Isaiah 6:3

and chant "Holy, holy, holy Lord God of hosts. Heaven and earth are full of your glory."

The Angel Proclaims Good News to the Shepherds (Luke 2:10)

"The angel said to them, 'Do not be afraid *(me phobeisthe); for see (idou gar),* I am bringing you good news *(euangelizomai hymin)* of great joy *(charan megalen)* for all the people *(hetis estai panti to lao)'"* (2:10).

If every celestial manifestation inspires awe and fear, the standard reassurance an angelic messenger delivers is "Do not fear." This is found in both the Old and New Testaments. To focus only on the New Testament, where we find more than a dozen examples in the gospels alone, we see that Zechariah was the acting priest of service in his division's turn to enter the sanctuary of the Lord to burn incense before God (1:5–25). The angel said to him, "Do not be afraid *(me phobou)"* (1:13a).

In the city of Nazareth, the angel was sent to a virgin betrothed to a man named Joseph. The angel greeted her as favored one and told her that the Lord was with her. The angel Gabriel said to Mary, "Do not be afraid *(me phobou)"* (1:30a).

Jesus told Simon Peter to go out into the deep water and lower his nets for a haul (5:1–11). So they did and swept in so great a number of fish that their nets were beginning to burst (5:6). When Simon saw this, he fell at the knees of Jesus, telling Jesus to depart from him, for he was a sinful man. Jesus said to Simon Peter, "Do not be afraid *(me phobou);* from now on you will be catching people *(anthropous,* human beings, men and women)" (5:10).

When we sense our unworthiness, it is natural to be afraid, and just as natural to seek, and be grateful for, the reassurance that all is well. In the Gospel according to Luke, the event being announced was characterized as bringing great joy (2:10b). This joy was for all the people (2:10c).

The birth, childhood, and mission of John the Baptist as a holy prophet was for the whole region of the Jordan (1:5–25). Likewise, Mary was told that her child would "reign over the [entire] house of Jacob forever" (1:33).

The Savior Is Born in the City of David

The angel Gabriel said to the shepherds of the flock in the countryside of Bethlehem, "to you *(hymin)* is born *(etechthe)* this day *(semeron,* today) in the city of David *(en polei Dauid)* a Savior *(Soter),* who is *(hos estin)* the Messiah *(Christos,* Christ), the Lord *(Kyrios)*" (Luke 2:11).

A birth has taken place that will benefit the shepherds and all who hear the good news. Today, the mention is clearly to the actual birth of Jesus. The "city of David" was Bethlehem of Judah, five miles south of Jerusalem, as immortalized in Micah's poem prophesied about a shepherd king from Bethlehem (5:2, 4):

> *But you, O Bethlehem of Ephrathah*
> *who are one of the little clans of Judah,*
> *from you shall come forth for me*
> *one who is to rule in Israel.*
> *And he shall stand and feed (poimanei) his flock*
> *(to poimnion autou)*
> *in the strength of the LORD,*
> *in the majesty of the name of the LORD his God.*

The Savior, the Christ (Messiah), the Lord (2:11c)

The Savior. Luke is the first evangelist to ascribe the title of savior to Jesus (2:11c),[7] the only synoptic, in fact, to do so. John uses it once, where it is found on the lips of the Samaritans who tell the woman: "We have heard for ourselves, and we know that this is truly the Savior *(Soter)* of the world." It had often been applied to Yahweh. Mary, for example, enshrined it in her canticle, the Magnificat: "My soul magnifies the Lord, and my spirit rejoices in God (Yahweh) my Savior" (1:47).

Luke had applied the title to Jesus in the Canticle of Zechariah, the Benedictus *(eulogetos):* "He has raised up a mighty *(keras,* the horn) savior *(soterias,* of the salvation) for us in the house *(en oiko)* of his servant David *(Dauid paidos* [slave, servant] *autou)*" (1:69).

The righteous and devout Simeon, with the child Jesus in his arms, sang the *Nunc Dimittis,* "Master, now you are dismissing your servant in peace, according to your word; for my eyes have seen your salvation *(to soterion sou)*" (2:29–30).

Salvation was a rather fluid concept then. It embraced a number of meanings, all of which implied a sense of wholeness and well-being. When applied to Jesus, it also included a proper relationship with God, implying the forgiveness of sins. Later, through the story of Zaccheus, we can perhaps glimpse how Luke understood this. In choosing to go to the home of Zaccheus, Jesus aroused the ire of the Pharisees, who scornfully muttered that he had gone to the house of a sinner to eat. The concluding statement of Jesus here is telling: "The Son of Man came to seek out and save the lost" (19:10).

This effectively answered two questions posed earlier in the Gospel: "Who, then, can be saved?" (18:26), or who can enter the kingdom of God (see 18:24–25). In gratitude for Jesus' reaching out to him, Zacchaeus promised restitution and to give half of his goods to the poor, showing exemplary repentance. He was no longer a sinner. Jesus would continue to exercise this same ministry in the Eucharist, when he invites sinners who have accepted the call to repentance to his table.

The Messiah. The second title given Jesus by the angel was the *Christ* (Messiah). Luke used Christ *(ho Christos)* as a title[8] 24 times (Luke 2:11c, 26; 3:15; 4:41; 9:20; Acts 2:31, 36; 3:18, 20; 4:26;

5:42). The title was used so frequently that it became associated with the primary name (Jesus) as a secondary name (Christ) in many Luke-Acts texts, just as it is for us today.

The name means "anointed." It was used in the Old Testament to indicate mainly the kings of Israel but also the priests. These were seen to have been appointed by God, and therefore deserving of protection and respect. They were the means whereby the justice and goodness of God would be visited upon his people. As the gap between the ideals of the Davidic kingship and historical reality widened, however, this royal language and imagery came to be applied to a future king whose reign would be characterized by justice, security, and peace. By New Testament times, it denoted an expected or hoped-for savior that God would raise up in order to realize all the expectations that came with the institution of kings in Israel.

There was no unified or single understanding of what Messiah meant when Jesus was born, though most thought of one who would restore the luster of the Davidic reign. And the idea that the Messiah would suffer was obviously difficult to reconcile with the notion of a triumphant Messiah. When Peter was able to proclaim that Jesus was the Messiah, Jesus immediately began to teach that the Messiah would have to suffer, and each time that he did so, even the disciples did not understand what he was saying (see, for example, Mark 8:31–33; 9:30-32; 10:32–45). Luke even tells us that just before the Ascension of Jesus into heaven, the disciples asked, "Lord, is this the time when you will restore the kingdom to Israel?" (Acts 1:6).

The Lord. The third title the angel gave Jesus was *Lord (Kyrios)*. The term Lord appears in Luke-Acts for both Yahweh and Jesus. In Luke-Acts, the Lord is the most frequently used title of Jesus, occurring almost twice as often as Christ;[9] it continued to be used as a real title, but did not become part of the name, as Christ did.

This is basically an honorific title, used of a king, a god—a husband even—since as a polite form of address it can be addressed to any superior. It was frequently applied to Yahweh, especially in the psalms. Since the name Yahweh was not pronounced out of reverence, even when it was written in the biblical text, *Lord* was said instead. When the Septuagint translated the Hebrew text into Greek, Lord was used instead of God's proper name. In respect for the sensitivities of our Jewish brethren, this is still the custom in our Lectionaries.

When used for Jesus in the gospels, Lord is often simply a term of respect and would have meant little more than "sir." In the epistles, however, we see that the early Church applied this term to Jesus in a much deeper sense. Note the famous hymn found in Philippians 2:6–11, which concludes with the ringing declaration: ". . . that at the name of Jesus, every knee should bend, in heaven and on earth and under the earth, and every tongue confess that Jesus Christ is Lord, to the glory of God the Father" (Philippians 2:10–11). This exaltation of Jesus came with his Resurrection to the right hand of God. The purpose of his life was that he might become Lord of the living and the dead (see Romans 14:8–9).

Luke uses the term in the prologue in this theological sense. In a sense, he retrojects the understanding of Jesus that followed the Resurrection. This stems from the conviction by Luke that, as the first sermon of Peter makes clear: ". . . let the entire house of Israel know with certainty that God has made him both Lord and Messiah, this Jesus whom you crucified" (Acts 2:36). The angel, however, is only echoing the cry of Elizabeth at the visitation, "And why has this happened to me, that the mother of my Lord comes to me?" (1:43).

Raymond Brown suggests that the primary background for the angelic announcement is the passage from Isaiah 9:6: "For a child has been born for us, a son given to us; authority rests upon his shoulders; and he is named Wonderful Counselor, Mighty God,

Everlasting Father, Prince of Peace." For these titles, Luke substitutes three titles of Jesus that had become an integral part of the Christian tradition.[10] This was the core of the Christian *kerygma*, and it was indeed good news for all who heard and accepted it. The announcement is made, says Brown, in the form of an imperial proclamation: "This day—" is a bold statement that a new era in human history has begun.

A Sign for Shepherds (Luke 2:12)

The angel said, "This will be a sign *(to semeion)* for you: you will find *(heuresete)* a child *(brephos)* wrapped in bands of cloth *(esparganomenon)* and lying *(keimenon)* in a manger *(en phatne)*" (2:12).[11]

Signs can be objects perceivable by the senses, and of these there are many. They can also be a means to establish a certainty that was not previously present. In this sense, they will confirm the truth of a message or serve to strengthen faith. That is especially true when the sign is seen as coming from God. The promise of a sign gives the shepherds the confidence to go to Bethlehem to see for themselves what the angel had announced. They would then become signs to Mary and Joseph of the extent of God's concern for his people. Signs abound in the Old Testament. In Exodus 3:12, God gave a sign to Moses:

> *I will be with you and this shall be the sign* (to semeion) *for you that it is I who sent you: when you have brought the people out of Egypt you shall worship God on this mountain.*

In 1 Samuel 2:34, the Lord God specifies that the fate of Eli's two sons, Hophni and Phinehas, would be a sign *(to semeion)* to him, "both of them shall die on the same day."

The sign given to Zechariah by the angel, in answer to Zechariah's question, "How shall I know this (to be true)? For I am an old man and my wife is advanced in years" (1:18) was that, despite their old age, Elizabeth would conceive.

Even to Mary, who did not ask for a sign, the angel Gabriel said, "And now, your relative Elizabeth in her old age has also conceived a son; and this is the sixth month for her who was said to be barren" (1:36). The sign, again, was Elizabeth's old age.

The angel Gabriel expressed most clearly for the shepherds the *sign* whereby they would recognize their Savior, Messiah, and Lord. They would find an infant wrapped in swaddling clothes and lying in a manger. As was shown in the previous chapter, the swaddling clothes are an indication of the true humanity of the child. This corresponds more with Jesus' being the Messiah or Christ. As the Gospels make clear, the Messiah would have to suffer and die, as do all human beings. In Luke 9:20–22, after Peter is able to proclaim that Jesus is the Messiah sent by God, Jesus begins to correct their notion of the Messiah as one who would restore the earthly kingdom of David by leading a revolution against the Romans. "The Son of Man," he told them, "must undergo great suffering, and be rejected by the elders, the chief priests, and the scribes, and be killed, and on the third day be raised" (9:22).

When Mary placed her son in the manger, she offered him, as he would one day be on the cross, as nourishment for God's flock, a gesture which summarized the role she accepted with her fiat: "Here am I, the servant of the Lord" (1:38a). The manger thus reveals the entire life, presence, and teaching of Jesus as nourishment for the universal Church. In Acts 20:28–29, Luke identifies the flock with the Church. The manger image refers to the table from which God would feed his flock.

The manger, or rather the laying of Jesus in a manger, indicates that he is truly Lord. Jesus will be Lord because, by dying for us, he was raised to new life, a life that he now enjoys at the right hand of God. From there he will come again "in his glory and the glory of the Father and of the holy angels" (9:26). Signs, in this sense, are not road maps as much as proofs that the message being announced is true.

A Multitude of the Heavenly Host Praising God
(Luke 2:13–14)

"And suddenly there was (2:13a) with the angel a multitude of the heavenly host (*stratias ouraniou,* army of heaven), (2:13b) praising God and saying, 'Glory *(doxa)* to God *(Theo)* in the highest heaven *(en hypsistois),* and on earth *(kai epi ges)* peace *(eirene)* among those *(en anthropois)* whom he favors *(eudokias)!'*" (2:14).

The prophet Micaiah had spoken of this angelic host: "Therefore hear the word of the LORD: I saw the Lord sitting on his throne, with all the host of heaven (*pasa he stratia* [all the army] *tou ouranou*) standing beside him to the right and to the left of him" (1 Kings 22:19). The idea is that this host, this army, is too numerous to count.

Luke refers to the glory of God in heaven.[12] When the angel of the Lord appeared to the shepherds, "the glory *(doxa)* of the Lord shone around them." The bright manifestation of glorious light was expressive of the presence of the invisible God. Now the relation could be made to the majesty of God visible in a little child.

In the Old Testament, if holiness is an attribute of the transcendence of God, glory is a manifestation of his immanence. We sing this in our eucharistic celebrations, which have taken over the hymn of Isaiah 6:3: "Holy, holy, holy Lord is the Lord of hosts; the whole earth is full of his glory. Heaven and earth are full of your glory." In the Bible, all glory is viewed as coming from God. It is caused by him and exists for him in all things. As Saint Paul exclaims, "To him be the glory forever. Amen" (Romans 11:36).

It did not take long for the glory that came to Christ in his Resurrection to be retrojected into his earthly life. In John, the entire ministry of Jesus is seen as a reflection of the glory of God.

The New Testament then applied to Jesus the glory the Old Testament reserved to God alone. The letter to the Hebrews ends with an exhortation that we carry out everything that is pleasing in the sight of God "through Jesus Christ, to whom be the glory forever and ever. Amen" (Hebrews 13:21).

The angels then wish peace as the gifts God presents to the world. The way in which the phrase "and on earth peace" in the brief angelic hymn is understood depends on the exact meaning of the last words in the verse, translated in the NRSV as "among those whom he favors!"

Historically, this verse has received two other translations. The first is "on earth peace, [and] good will towards men"; the second is "and on earth peace among men of good will." Fitzmyer and Brown seem to have agreed that the better translation is "and on earth peace for people whom he [God] favors." This seems logical, for we would not expect the angels to be speaking of the good will exhibited here on earth, especially when Bethlehem had just rejected Jesus! Nor should we expect them to be saying that human good will was necessary for God to offer us his peace. Peace comes because God has favored us, because in his goodness, God has "so loved the world that he sent his only Son" (John 3:16).

Reflection on the Shepherds and the Angels

The reading from the Gospel according to Luke for the Mass at midnight on Christmas consists of the narratives of the birth of Jesus, Mary's son and the firstborn Son of God, climaxing with the angelic hymn: "Glory to God in the highest heaven, and on earth peace among those whom he favors!"

Given all the emphasis on the Davidic lineage of Jesus, the pastoral scene Luke depicts in 2:8–14 is appropriate. David had been the shepherd king of Israel. Again, divine splendor enveloped humble humanity. The heavenly message came to shepherds. God chooses the weak to make them strong. Or, as Mary said in her Magnificat: "He [God] has looked with favor on his lowly servant. He has brought down the powerful from their thrones and lifted up the lowly" (1:48, 52).

The message of redemption was not given to Herod, who reigned over Israel, or to Caesar Augustus on his throne in Rome. Neither did it come to the Sanhedrin or the chief priests, nor to the Pharisees. It was not the great ones of the earth who were so blessed; rather, it was shepherds watching over their flocks at night. How consoling a message this must be for so many who are poor and disadvantaged! Those who lack status in this world need not despair that God will neglect them as have the powerful.

The angelic manifestation that accompanies the glory of God directs attention to the good news that a Savior, who is both Christ (Messiah) and Lord, has been born (2:10–11). This short sentence summarizes early Christian catechesis. We are being told, even before the story of Jesus unfolds in the Gospel, what we can expect to find there. Jesus is the source of our salvation, of establishing a relationship of adoption between God and the human race. He will do this as a suffering Messiah, one who was willing to lay down his life for the flock. For this reason we can approach him with confidence, because he has become risen Lord, ever in heaven to intercede for us.

This is why the angels can sing of our being favored with the peace that God offers. God takes the initiative to right the balance that had been lost in our lives. This includes the sinfulness in our lives as well as the evil and selfish value system of the world. The lack of hospitality that Jesus found in Bethlehem is still a factor in our world. However, to those who accept Christ as their savior, and follow his way of life, it is possible to experience a peace such as the world cannot give. Those who read the Gospel according to Luke and turn to the Savior in their midst (2:12), those, that is, on whom the favor of God rests, will enjoy nothing short of the peace God offers. Such is the way the glory of God is manifested by those whom he favors.

"Glory to God in the highest heaven!"

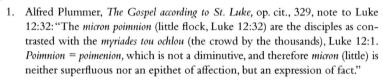

1. Alfred Plummer, *The Gospel according to St. Luke,* op. cit., 329, note to Luke 12:32: "The *micron poimnion* (little flock, Luke 12:32) are the disciples as contrasted with the *myriades tou ochlou* (the crowd by the thousands), Luke 12:1. *Poimnion* = *poimenion,* which is not a diminutive, and therefore *micron* (little) is neither superfluous nor an epithet of affection, but an expression of fact."

2. Luke Timothy Johnson wrote in Acts 20:28 in note on: "*to shepherd the Church of God:* The verb *poimainein* carries forward the image of the flock and the shepherd, and points to Luke's understanding of the presbyterate/episcopate and an administration position" in *The Acts of the Apostles,* Sacra Pagina 5 (Collegeville, Minnesota: The Liturgical Press, 1992), 363.

3. Edward Gordon Selwyn writes in 1 Peter 5:2 in note on: "*poimanate,* tend: The word is classical (Homer, Hesiod, Euripides, Plato, Theocritus), and includes the whole of a shepherd's care for his flock, and not feeding only" in *The First Epistle of St. Peter* (London: MacMillan and Co. Ltd., 1964), 229.

4. E. G. Selwyn wrote in 1 Peter 5:4 in note on: "*archipoimenos* a beautiful word, *hapax legomenon* in Scripture, but probably in the vernacular of the period while St. Peter's word *archipoimen* underlines its relationship to those who have pastoral charge in the Christian ministry. In relation to them Christ is the *chief shepherd,* set over them yet sharing their function," ibid., 231–232.

5. "Ignatius to the Romans," The Apostolic Fathers, with an English translation by Kirsopp Lake, in 2 volumes (Cambridge, Massachusetts: Harvard University Press, 1959), I:236–237.

6. "Ignatius to the Philadelphians," ibid., I: 240–241.

7. The title savior is from the Roman imperial period of Pompey. It was applied to the emperors, Caesar Augustus, Caligula, Nero, Domitian and Hadrian, who where worshipped as saviors, as were also the gods, the physicians, the philosophers, and the statesmen.

8. The title, Christ (Messiah), is acquired from Palestinian Judaism. Joseph A. Fitzmyer, SJ, *The Gospel according to Luke I–IX,* op. cit., 197–198: Its origin is found in the Old Testament (Hebrew) use of *masiah,* "anointed one," which was translated in the LXX as *christos.* Both the Hebrew root *msh* and Greek

chriein mean "anoint." In the Old Testament, the anointing did not have a uni-vocal significance, but the title was generically used of certain historical persons regarded as anointed agents of Yahweh for the service or protection of his people, Israel. It was usually applied to kings of Israel (Saul, David, and successors on the Davidic throne), but at times it was applied to others as well (the high priest, even Cyrus, the Persian king).

9. J. A. Fitzmyer, *The Gospel according to Luke I–IX*, ibid., 409–410, in the note on Luke 2:11: *the Messiah, the Lord*. Two further titles are added to "Savior" in the angelic announcement, traditional titles inherited by Luke from the early Palestinian Christian community before him, but now predicated by him of Jesus at his very birth Luke actually writes here *christos kyrios*, two anarthrous nominatives. This is the reading in the best Greek mss. But some ancient versions read christos kyriou, "the Lord's Messiah."

10. R. E. Brown, *The Birth of the Messiah*, 434–435.

11. R. E. Brown, *The Birth of the Messiah*, op. cit., 403, in the note on Luke 2:12, says that the sign will be a personal one. He translates this verse as the angel saying *"your sign."* Literally, "a sign to you." This reading is supported by Codex Vaticanus. Most other manuscripts, however, including Codex Bezae, read "*the* sign for you." The definite article appears in Old Testament parallels. The angel is giving more than a roadmap as to how to find the baby. He is saying how they will realize that he is truly their savior.

12. J. A. Fitzmyer, *The Gospel according to Luke I–IX*, op. cit., in the note of Luke 2:14: "*Glory to God in highest heaven.* Lit. 'glory in (the) highest to God.' This hymnic formula is not found as such in the OT, but it is based on phrases about 'giving glory' *(doxan didonai)* to God, i.e., honoring him, in such passages as Baruch 2:17–18; I Esdras 9:8; 4 Maccabees 1:12," 410.

The Visit of the Shepherds

When the angels had left them and gone into heaven, the shepherds said to one another, "Let us go now to Bethlehem and see this thing that has taken place, which the Lord has made known to us."

So they went with haste and found Mary and Joseph, and the child lying in the manger. When they saw this, they made known what had been told them about this child; and all who heard it were amazed at what the shepherds told them.

But Mary treasured all these words and pondered them in her heart. The shepherds returned, glorifying and praising God for all they had heard and seen, as it had been told them. (Luke 2:15–20)

It is one thing to hear the word of God and quite another to put it into practice. The greatest praise that Luke can give to Mary is not that she was the mother of God, but that her greatness lay in the fact that she heard the word of God and kept it (11:28). "My mother and my brothers," Jesus told us, "are those who hear the word of God and do it" (8:21). In the shepherds, we can see from the beginning those who not only heard the word of God, but acted upon it.

The angelic message was a promise of "good news of great joy for all the people" (2:10). This good news was embodied in a baby, one still wrapped in swaddling cloths and lying in a manger.

Babies were born all the time, and they were all wrapped in bands of cloth. But angels did not herald their births, nor were they to be found lying in a manger. And so the shepherds decide to act on the message and see for themselves what the angel announced. They then leave to proclaim the Good News to others, and to praise and thank God for having revealed this to them and used them as his instruments of proclamation.

The visit to Bethlehem was thus an epiphany for the shepherds,[1] a manifestation of God's loving kindness visited upon his people. Mary, of course, treasured all these things in her heart. She models for us a contemplative reflection on the word and action of God in our lives.

The Angels Left and Returned to Heaven

"When (*kai* [and] *egeneto* [it happened] *hos* [when]) the angels *(hoi angeloi)* had left them *(ap' auton)* and [had left] gone *(apelthon)* into heaven *(eis ton ouranon)*" (2:15a).

The angels returned to heaven, the dwelling place of God. We are told in the first words of the Bible that God created the heavens (Genesis 1:1). From Old Testament times people believed that God lived in heaven, along with the heavenly host (see 1 Kings 22:19 ff.). Because God dwells in heaven, conceived as existing above the dome of the sky, hands are lifted up in prayer (Exodus 9:29), and mountains on earth are felt to bring us that much closer to God. God is also asked to look down on us from heaven (Deuteronomy 26:15). Enthroned in the heavens on high, God rules the earth (Psalm 113:5–6).

These concepts are also found in the New Testament. Heaven as the dwelling place of God is firmly fixed and often noted by Luke, who uses the word heaven more than a dozen times. It is from heaven that Jesus hears the voice of God and the Holy Spirit comes to him to prepare him for his public ministry.

Now when all the people were baptized, and when Jesus also had been baptized and was praying, the heaven *(ton ouranon)* was opened, and the Holy Spirit descended upon him in bodily form like a dove. And a voice came from heaven *(ex ouranou):* "You are my Son, the Beloved; with you I am well pleased" (3:21–22).

As the dwelling place of God, revelation comes from heaven. Thus, the angels in the infancy narrative speak with divine authority. The baptism of John is also from God, as we see in the trap Jesus set for those who were trying to discredit him: "Did the baptism of John come from heaven, or is it of human origin?" (Luke 19:4).

Heaven, for Luke, is also the place where the just will be rewarded for their fidelity. In the Lukan version of the Beatitudes, we find the following:

> *Blessed are you when people hate you, and when they exclude you, revile you, and defame you on account of the Son of Man. Rejoice in that day and leap for joy, for surely your reward is great in heaven. (6:22–23)*

Luke uses the heavens *(ouranoi)* in the plural form, as when Jesus says:

> *People will faint from fear and foreboding of what is coming upon the world, for the powers of the heavens* (ton ouranon) *will be shaken. Then they will see "the Son of Man coming in a cloud" with power and great glory. (21:26–27)*

There seems to be little difference between the singular and plural forms. Classical Greek would use only the singular. Under the influence of Hebrew, however (Genesis 1:1 uses the plural), the plural form is sometimes used. This reflects biblical faith that God created the entire universe. The plural would indicate the dominion God has over all of creation. He does not share creation with other gods.

The Shepherds Said to One Another, "Let us Go"

"When the angels had left them and gone into heaven, the shepherds *(hoi poimenes)* said *(elaloun)* to one another *(pros allelous)*, 'Let us go *(Dielthomen)* now *(heos)* to Bethlehem *(Bethleem)* and see *(kai idomen)* this thing *(to rhema touto)* that has taken place *(to gegonos)*, which the Lord *(ho ho Kyrios)* has made known *(egnorisen)* to us *(hemin)*'" (Luke 2:15).

In the scriptures we are told to be attentive to God's word *(logos)*. When that word is expressed in some definitive manner, it can be expressed, as it is here, by *rhema,* (thing, word, event), although the LXX treats them both as synonyms.[2] In the Gospel, the expressions "word," "word of God," and "word of the Lord" are used synonymously. As it is used in Luke 2:15, it denotes Jesus in the manger; however, it also evokes what the will of God will one day accomplish through Jesus. His will be a message of grace and reconciliation; it is for our life. John summed this up in with Jesus saying, "I am the way, and the truth, and the life. No one comes to the Father except through me" (14:6).

God's word is not simply something spoken. It is active and effective. When God spoke, the world was created. It sufficed for God to say, "Let there be light," for there to be light. Jesus often healed by the power of his word. Not that there was anything magical about the words he used, rather, his word itself had authority. This is noted in the Gospel according to Luke as well. "They were astounded at his teaching, because he spoke with authority" (4:32), and also "They were all amazed and kept saying to one another, 'What kind of utterance is this? For with authority and power he commands the unclean spirits, and out they come!'" (4:36).

Although an angel said the words to the shepherds and, even earlier, to Mary (1:26), Luke can refer to them as from the Lord: "And blessed is she who believed that there would be a fulfillment of what was spoken to her by the Lord"(1:45). Like Mary, the shepherds were not content to simply hear the word. They decided to follow it: "let us go now to Bethlehem to see this thing that has taken place." In their simplicity, they did not question, nor did they ignore. Rather, they left their flocks and acted upon what they had heard. Luke surely sees them as models of true discipleship, *for they heard the word of God and acted upon it.*

The Shepherds Went with Haste and Found the Child Lying in the Manger

Luke adds a detail to the journey of the shepherds to Bethlehem. They were eager to follow the instruction of the angel and find the child. "So they went *(kai elthon)* with haste and found *(speusantes kai aneuron)* Mary and Joseph *(ten te Mariam kai ton Ioseph),* and the child *(kai to brephos)* lying *(keimenon)* in the manger *(en te phatne)*" (Luke 2:16).

The shepherds came in haste, literally "hurrying, *(speusantes).*" In the Gospel according to Luke, we see others hurrying to do God's bidding. The Virgin Mary set out to visit Elizabeth and traveled "with haste *(meta spoudes)* to a Judean town in the hill country" (1:39). To Zacchaeus, the tax collector, Jesus said, "'Zacchaeus, hurry *(speusas)* and come down; for I must stay at your house today.' So he hurried *(speusas)* down and was happy to welcome him" (19:5–6). There was no holding back, no resistance. Rather, they were eager to follow a message that they realized came from heaven.

In Bethlehem, the shepherds, just as they had been told, "found Mary and Joseph and the child lying in the manger." The angel had told the shepherds not to be afraid, for it was a message of great joy that was being proclaimed to them for all the people. The sign that he gave them was that they would find the child wrapped in bands of cloth and lying in a manger. There is no suggestion that they had to look around for such a child to know whether they had found the right one. Seemingly, they were told exactly where to go. It is not like the story told in Matthew, where Herod, having no such sign, had to kill all the male children under two to make sure he had the right one.

The swaddling bands that were mentioned would have been no help in finding the Savior. Because there was an assumption that swaddling would make bones grow straight, every child was swaddled. The real sign to them was the manger. It gave an insight into the significance of this birth. As mentioned in chapter two, the manger was indicative of God's desire to feed his people. Jesus is there, offered as food for the life of the world. The window in the Cathedral of Chartres depicting Jesus, not in a manger but on an altar, captures this insight. For that is surely where we can find him today.

The Shepherds Made the Message Known

"When *(de)* they (the shepherds) saw *(idontes)* this, they made known *(egnorisan)* what *(peri tou rhematos)* had been told *(tou lalethentos)* them *(autois)* about *(peri)* this child *(tou paidiou toutou)*" (2:17).

"When the shepherds saw this," they remembered what the angel had told them about a sign, a child lying in a manger. That was the sign that had been given them. And that is what they found, confirming in their minds the truth of the message from the angel. The manger was more than a convenient place where Mary could lay Jesus down. It was a sign, part of the Gospel message for all who had eyes to see.

"The shepherds made known,"[3] apparently to Mary and Joseph, although it is surely possible that others were present. Here they act as messengers of the Good News; they were evangelizers. It is one thing to hear the voice of God and to respond to that voice personally. But they shared with others what they had heard and seen. Fidelity to the word of God requires that we share it with others. This idea did not originate with Luke. It characterized Christian understanding of the Gospel. A generation before Luke wrote, Saint Paul told the people of Corinth: "for an obligation is laid on me, and woe to me if I do not proclaim the gospel!" (1 Corinthians 9:16). This does not, of course, mean that such evangelizing will be understood or appreciated. Acts 26 recounts how the Roman official Festus thought Paul showed signs of madness.

> *Festus exclaimed, "You are out of your mind, Paul! Too much learning is driving you insane!" (Acts 26:24) Paul said: "Indeed the king knows about these things, and to him I speak freely (boldly); for I am certain that none of these things has escaped his notice, for this was not done in a corner." (Acts 26:26)*[4]

The shepherds, however, are shown as understanding the sign and making the event known, even as it was told them. Unlike many other efforts at evangelization, the shepherds' words were better received than many others.

The prospect of hostile receptions, beatings, imprisonment, and even death did not deter Paul from spreading the Good News. In Acts 20:22–23, he explains that he is bound to tell of Christ. "And now, as a captive to the Spirit, I am on my way to Jerusalem, not knowing what will happen to me there, except that the Holy Spirit testifies to me in every city that imprisonments and persecutions are waiting for me."

Peter and John, too, explained that they had to proclaim the Good News of the Messiah. Standing before the Jewish Council after being arrested, they said, "we cannot keep from speaking about what we have seen and heard" (Acts 4:20).

Astonishment at What the Shepherds Said to Them

"And *(kai)* all (pantes) who heard *(hoi akousantes)* it were amazed *(ethaumasan)* at what the shepherds *(hypo ton poimenon)* told *(peri ton lalethenton)* them *(pros autous)*" (2:18).

In the aftermath of the circumcision and naming of John the Baptist, the same phrase was used, "All *(pantes)* who heard *(hoi akousantes)* them pondered them and said, 'What then will this child become?' For, indeed, the hand of the Lord was with him" (1:66). In this instance, we were prepared by the information that had been presented to the intended audience: "Her neighbors and relatives heard *(ekousan)* that the Lord had shown his great mercy to her, and they rejoiced with her" (1:58).

What is this amazement? It is a sense of awe, faced with the manifestation of the numinous, the divine. We are dealing here with a religious experience of someone who has come face to face with what transcends human possibilities and must therefore be ascribed to God. Psalm 96:3 states, "Declare his glory among the nations, his marvelous works among all the peoples."

In the New Testament we often see people marveling when witnessing miracles. Luke 8:25 states that the disciples were amazed when Jesus stilled the storm on the Lake of Genesareth. In the infancy narrative of Luke, we see that when Zechariah was silenced and unable to talk because of his disbelief, the people "wondered *(ethaumazon)*[5] at his delay in the sanctuary" (1:21). And when it came time for the circumcision and the relatives objected to the name John, Zechariah asked for a tablet and wrote, "His name is John. And all of them were amazed *(ethaumasan)*" (1:63).

This same religious awe is seen in those who hear the shepherds: "And all who heard it were amazed *(ethaumasan,* wondered, surprised, astonished) at what the shepherds told them" (2:18). This awe is also experienced when the child is presented in the Temple, and Simeon takes Jesus in his arms and praises God:

Master, now you are dismissing your servant in peace,
according to your word;
for my eyes have seen your salvation,
which you have prepared in the presence of all peoples,
a light for revelation to the Gentiles
and for glory to your people Israel. (2:29–32)

Joseph and Mary "were amazed *(thaumazontes)* at what was being said about him" (2:33). We have here an extension of the revelation received at the birth of Jesus. Jesus would be a Savior not only for Israel but for the Gentiles as well. We can see here how the infancy narratives prepare the way for themes that will be developed in the gospel proper. The second part of the oracle Simeon proclaims is somewhat starker. We are reminded that for many in Israel, Jesus will be a sign that is rejected (2:34). Good news is not always well received.

Mary Kept All These Things, Pondering Them in Her Heart

"But *(de)* Mary *(he Mariam)* treasured *(syneterei)* all *(panta)* these words *(ta rhemata tauta,* things) and pondered *(symballousa)* them *(autes)* in her heart *(en te kardia)*" (2:19).

In Bethlehem, when the shepherds related everything they had been told about the child, Mary treasured all these words."[6] While the shepherds proclaimed what had been told them and what they had seen to one and all, we are told that all marveled, but only Mary is said to have treasured all these things. Joseph is not even mentioned, for it is Mary who has center stage in the Gospel according to Luke. Raymond Brown suggests that perhaps Luke had in mind the reaction of the audience in the parable of the seed. There, the seed that fell on rock was compared to those who "when they hear the word, receive it with joy. But these have no root; they believe only for a while and in a time of testing fall away" (8:13). Mary, of course, would be like those who, "when they hear the word, hold it fast in an honest and good heart, and bear fruit with patient endurance" (8:15). This seems likely in view of the passage that comes only four verses later: "My mother and my brothers are those who hear the word of God and do it" (8:21).

The ability of Mary to treasure, keep in memory, and ponder, or, as the verb *symballein* literally means, "tossing together in her heart," is presented in the Gospel as a characteristic of her response to the good news. When the angel appeared to Mary at the Annunciation, she was "much perplexed by his words and *pondered* what sort of greeting this might be" (1:29). When Jesus was brought to the Temple at 12 years of age and remained behind, he answered his parents' query with the enigmatic words, "Did you not know that I must be in my Father's house? . . . His mother *treasured* all these things in her heart" (2:49, 51).

The Shepherds Went Back Glorifying and Praising God

"The shepherds *(hoi poimenes)* returned *(hypestrepsan)*, glorifying *(doxazontes)* and *(kai)* praising *(ainountes)* God *(ton theon)* for *(epi)* all *(pasin)* they *(hois)* had heard *(ekousan)* and *(kai)* seen *(eidon)*, as *(kathos)* it had been told *(elalethe)* them *(pros autous)*" (2:20).

Having seen Mary, Joseph, and the child lying in the manger, the shepherds returned to their flocks "glorifying and praising God." As symbolic figures, when sharing the good news with those in Bethlehem, the shepherds prefigured early Church leaders spreading the gospel. Now, returning home, they represent more the average Christian who should praise and glorify God for the wonders of his creation and the marvelous things he has done for them, especially for the salvation they have received in Christ.

To give God glory is not to give him anything he did not already have, but simply to acknowledge publicly the recognition that is his due. It extols what is already a reality. Psalm 96:8 says,

"Ascribe to the Lord the glory due his name." All that is needed is that we recognize the author of all good gifts.

The following verses illustrate this recognition in the psalms.

"The heavens are telling the glory of God;
and the firmament proclaims his handiwork." (Psalm 19:1)

The heavens proclaim his righteousness,
and all the people behold his glory. (Psalm 97:6)

The voice of the LORD causes the oaks to whirl, and strips the
*   forest bare;*
and in his Temple all say, "Glory!" (Psalm 29:3, 9)

Who is the king of glory?
*   The LORD, strong and mighty, the Lord, mighty in battle."*
(Psalm 24:8)

Reflection on the Visit of the Shepherds

The shepherds' decision to act on the angelic message is important. As Luke makes clear in his account, it is not sufficient to hear the word of God; it must be acted on. This requires faith, of course, but also overcoming the tendency of inertia present in all of us. We are comfortable with our present understanding and relationship with God and prefer that nothing disturb it. The shepherds are models of those who, having been attentive to the word of God, allow it to change their lives.

Luke captures the faithfulness of the shepherds in noting that they not only went to Bethlehem, but that they hurried there. Theirs was an eagerness to do the will of God. And in Bethlehem they had a double function. First of all, they verified the sign the angel gave them: a child lying in a manger. Second, they proclaimed what they had been told. Sharing the revelation they had received, they became proclaimers of the Good News.

Luke presumes, of course, that the shepherds understood the sign. The understanding of and the continuation of the sign in the Church are possible only for those familiar with the life of Jesus. It is also important to note the link that Luke makes between the lack of hospitality in Bethlehem and the hospitality Christ offers us from the upper room and from the altars around the world. Luke knew how to prefigure what would eventuate in the Gospel. There was a marked contrast in the sign of the manger and the swaddling bands that wrapped the limbs of Jesus. His was a humble birth; he was rejected by his own city, the city of his ancestor David, and was born not in a palace but a stable. He was wrapped in bands of cloth like any child. His humanity was obvious. Yet his manger revealed something else: his ability to be our Savior and to feed his flock down through the ages. This was also a proclamation that Jesus was a Savior for the poor and lowly, those with whom God was well pleased (2:14).

If we ask what they saw and understood, we might suggest two things in particular. The first is that our human condition is wrapped up in God. The peak experiences that are ours are meant to illuminate the rest of our everyday lives. They are the beacon of light that comes from above to give direction and purpose to everything else that we do. The second thing they learned was that our fulfillment and happiness are not bound up with material things. The divine was manifested in weak human flesh. The setting of the birth of Jesus was simple and human. But the poverty was only of material things, not of the spirit. That made all the difference.

Realizing this, the shepherds proclaim the Good News to others and share the epiphany that they had been privileged to experience. The wonder that those hearing them may have felt was the sense of reverence and awe that overtakes a person in the presence of the sacred. Such a sense recognizes that the ways of God are not our ways. The ways of God are beyond our comprehension and imagination. Being open to the mystery of God and the way his presence touches our world is necessary in the spiritual life.

It was after proclaiming their message of "great joy" that the shepherds returned to their flocks, back to the humdrum routines of husbandry and eking out a daily living. We are told that they did so while praising and glorifying God. Actually, we know nothing about what happened to them after they returned. They pass from the pages of biblical history. But, as Raymond Brown notes, "there has now begun a praise and glory of God on earth echoing the praise and glory of God by the heavenly host."[7] However, the real task of proclaiming the apostolic faith, he adds, was to begin only later, with the public ministry of Christ, especially after his Resurrection from the dead.

Despite the emphasis given the shepherds, Mary is the central figure in this pericope. It is she who recognizes the significance of the events and realizes that they require further thought and reflection. Through her pondering the meaning of the mysteries in her life, she discerns the will of God.

---

1. The Greek is *epiphaneia*, "appearance, manifestation"; *epi*, "to," and *phainein*, "manifest, appear, show." The epiphany is the manifestation of the Savior, Christ (Messiah), and Lord to the Jewish shepherds (Luke 2:15–20). The Epiphany (January 6) commemorates the manifestation of Christ (Messiah) to the Gentiles (Matthew 2:1–5) and was the earliest celebration of the birth of Christ in the Church.

2. Brown, *The Birth of the Messiah,* op. cit., 405. "This is a semitism: the Greek *rema* means 'word'; but here and in vss. 17, 19 it translates the double connotation of the Hebrew *dabar,* word, deed.' This is a deed that speaks."

3. I. Howard Marshall, *Commentary on Luke,* New International Greek Testament Commentary (Grand Rapids, Michigan: William B. Eerdmans, 1978), 113, in the note on Luke 2:17, "It is not absolutely clear to whom the shepherds made known the saying about the child. The wording, 'this child,' may imply that other people were already present with Mary and Joseph and the child."

4. Luke Timothy Johnson, *The Acts of the Apostles*, Sacra Pagina 5 (Collegeville, Minnesota: The Liturgical Press, 1992), 439, in the note on Acts 26:26: *For the king understands these things:* Paul turns from the obtuse Roman to the supposedly "expert" *(gnostes)* Agrippa, hoping that his "understanding" will win his approval. He, therefore, speaks with boldness *(parresiazomai),* showing himself in this respect once again thoroughly the philosopher/prophet, who even before hostility and skepticism proclaims his convictions (see Acts 2:29; 4:13, 29, 31; 9:27–28; 13:46; 14:3; 18:26; 19:8).

5. George Bertram, *"thauma, thaumazo, thaumasios, thaumastos," Theological Dictionary of the New Testament,* edited by Gerhard Kittel, translator and editor by Geoffrey W. Bromiley, Volume III, Th +K (Grand Rapids, Michigan: Wm. B. Eerdmans Publishing Company, 1965) 39: There are four occurrences of *thaumazein* in the infancy stories in Luke. The astonishment of the crowd at the extraordinarily long time that Zacharias tarried in the temple (Luke 1:21) serves as a literary device to prepare readers or hearers for the events that follow. Similarly, the astonishment of the crowd at the miraculous concurrence of the parents in naming the child (1:63) gives us a sense of the divine action in this story. Again, in Luke 2:18, 33 the astonishment of the hearers and parents is a means to prepare the ground for the fact that the story of Jesus has the character of revelation.

6. Brown, *The Birth of the Messiah,* New Updated Edition, op. cit., 406, in the note on Luke 2:19a: *kept with concern.* Luke uses the verb *synterein* here and *diaterein* in the parallel expression in 2:51. More than simple retention is meant, for *synterein* must be connected with the following verb *symballein* (Luke 2:19c): the difficult events that happened are to be retained in order to be interpreted correctly.

7. *The Birth of the Messiah,* 429.

The Circumcision
and Naming of Jesus

After eight days had passed, it was time to circumcise the child;
and he was called Jesus,
the name given by the angel before he was conceived in the womb.
(Luke 2:21)

Raymond Brown links this verse with the story of the birth of Jesus. Fitzmyer links it with the next pericope, in which Jesus is presented in the Temple. In any case, it serves as a bridge text between these major sections of the infancy narrative. Chronologically, it is closer to the birth, but it stands between that and the presentation.

After Eight Days

After *(hote)* eight days *(hemerai okto)* had passed *(eplesthesan)*, it was time to circumcise *(tou peritemein)* the child *(auton)*; and he was called *(eklethe to onoma autou)* Jesus *(Iesous)*, the name given by the angel before he was conceived in the womb (2:21).

Literally, Luke says, "when the eight days were fulfilled." The circumcision itself is not even mentioned, only the fact that the time had been fulfilled for him to be circumcised. The emphasis is on his naming. This was done when the times (days) were fulfilled. Luke uses the same expression to introduce the birth as well as the Presentation in the Temple:

It happened that while they were in the city of David that is called Bethlehem, "the time (hai hemerai) came (eplesthesan) for her to deliver her child." (2:6)

And then:

When "the time (hai hemerai) came for their purification" in keeping with the Law of Moses, they took him up to Jerusalem to present him to the Lord. (2:22)

There is a huge contrast between the narrative of the circumcision of John the Baptist and that of Jesus. The parents of John play major roles in the story, with Elizabeth's naming the child and Zechariah's recovering his speech and delivering the canticle, the Benedictus. Many relatives and friends were present for the circumcision of John the Baptist. For Jesus, it is not even specified that his parents were there, and the event is told in one sentence.[1]

The Child Jesus Was to Be Circumcised (Luke 2:21b)

The origins of circumcision are lost in antiquity. Seemingly, it began with Semitic peoples and migrated to Egypt more than four millennia ago. It would have been given different meanings by different people. The Hebrew understanding of the rite was quite rich.[2] For one thing, it gave a sense of national identity, setting them apart from the Philistines, Babylonians, Greeks, and Romans. A sign of the covenant that they enjoyed with God, circumcision incorporated an individual into the covenant community and was a source of blessings. It is akin to receiving the gift of salvation, much the same as Baptism incorporates a person into the body of Christ with all the blessings that provides. This is expressed in Colossians 2:11–13.

In him also you were circumcised with a spiritual circumcision, by putting off the body of the flesh in the circumcision of Christ;

when you were buried with him in baptism, you were also raised
with him through faith in the power of God, who raised him
from the dead. And when you were dead in trespasses and the
uncircumcision of your flesh, God made you alive together with
him, when he forgave us all our trespasses.

Circumcision as a religious obligation is mentioned early in Genesis. God said to Abraham that, because of the covenant:

Throughout your generations every male among you shall
be circumcised when he is eight days old (okto hemeron),
including the slave born in your house and the one bought with
your money from any foreigner who is not of your offspring.
(Genesis 17:12)

That this was a serious obligation is evidenced by the significance it acquired with the arrival of the Greeks, who found it abhorrent to deface the human body by circumcision. Antiochus Epiphanes IV forbade circumcision, and mothers and their circumcised babies were thrown from the walls of Jerusalem (1 Maccabees 1:48, 60–61; 2 Maccabees 6:10). Yet the observant continued to practice circumcision as a badge of their allegiance to Yahweh. This persecution of those who clung to their Jewish identity was one of the precipitating causes of the Maccabean revolt.

Because of its association with fidelity to God, circumcision took on metaphorical meanings. It indicated suitability for participating in what God was doing and an openness to doing his will. Moses complained that he had uncircumcised lips (Exodus 6:12, 30). Jeremiah spoke of uncircumcised ears that do not hear the warnings he is giving them (Jeremiah 6:10). In Jeremiah, circumcision is described as part of being faithful to God.

The days are coming, says the LORD, when I will attend to all
those who are circumcised only in the foreskin: Egypt, Judah,

Edom, the Ammonites, Moab and all those with shaven temples
who live in the desert. For all these nations are uncircumcised,
and all the house of Israel is uncircumcised in heart. (Jeremiah
9:25–26)

In the New Testament, Luke, despite all the problems with circumcision in the early Church depicted in the Acts of the Apostles, presents Mary and Joseph in the Gospel as observant, pious Jews. They are careful to fulfill the requirements of the Law. Through circumcision Jesus, the Christ (Messiah), is conformed to the Mosaic law: "But when the fullness of time *(to pleroma tou chronou)* had come, God sent his Son, born of a woman, born under the law *(hypo nomon)*"[3] (Galatians 4:4). We could already have suspected that this was the case from the words of Mary: "Be it done to me according to your word." The incarnate Son of God will be brought up in a solid piety, and educated to know the scriptures, as we can see from his familiarity with the Bible in his public ministry.

In the same way, circumcision of Jesus was but the first act of obedience to God and fulfillment of the law. As Jesus says during his ministry, "Do not think that I have come to abolish the law or the prophets; I have come not to abolish but to fulfill" (Matthew 5:17). The Fathers of the Church viewed the circumcision as the first drops of blood that Jesus shed for our redemption.

The New Testament saw the circumcision as yet another indication that Jesus was fully human. Saint Paul tells us that in sending Jesus,

God has done what the law, weakened (en ho esthenei) *by the*
flesh (dia tes sarkos), *could not do: by sending his own Son in*
the likeness of sinful flesh, and to deal with sin, he condemned
sin in the flesh." (Romans 8:3)

Mary and Joseph Gave the Name of Jesus (Luke 2:21c)

Mary and Joseph gave their child the name Jesus: "and he was called Jesus." Jesus in the Greek transliterates as *Iesous,* but the original Hebrew form of Jesus is *Yeshuah,* Joshua, or, more fully, *Yehoshua,* which means "Yahweh is salvation," "Yahweh saves," or "Yahweh will save." The name Jesus *(Iesous)* was quite popular among Jews in the Greek-Hellenistic times. The Latin transliterates it *Iesus* in the early Roman era.

Gabriel the archangel (in Hebrew, *gabri'el,* "El is strong"), said to Mary, "Do not be afraid, Mary, for you have found favor with God. And now, you will conceive in your womb and bear a son, and you will name him *(kaleseis to onoma autou)* Jesus *(Iesoun)*" (1:30–31). In the Gospel according to Matthew, Joseph is told by an angel not to be afraid to take the Virgin Mary as his wife. She will give birth to a son, and Joseph is "to name him Jesus." Because there is no indication that Luke knew of Matthew's account of the Gospel, this is an indication of the early Christian conviction that the naming of Jesus was determined on high.

Israel believed that names hold significance. Names establish identities. To change the name of a person—such as Jesus did with Peter—is to change the identity and role of the individual. Jesus' identity came from God. Because Jesus' name came from God, Mary was but the instrument God used in giving Jesus his name.

We can assume that Joseph was in agreement about the name, as it was considered the role of the father to name the child. We see that in the story of the naming of John the Baptist. Even though Elizabeth had told them that the name was John, it had to be confirmed by Zechariah (1:59–63). The role of Mary is highlighted here, as it will be throughout Luke. For Luke, she was the perfect mother, the perfect disciple.

Reflection on the Circumcision and Naming of Jesus

Most reflection on the circumcision comes from how it was understood in the New Testament and the early Church. Luke makes it a hinge between the Nativity and the Presentation in the Temple, as he portrays both events as times of divine revelation. We have the angelic messengers in the first and the prophetic voices of Simeon and Anna in the second. Both the messengers and voices indicate the future course of the life of Jesus.

Today, in our desire to know Jesus better, there is greater emphasis on the Jewish identity of Jesus. Here, from the beginning of the life of Jesus, we see his being reared in an authentically Jewish family, schooled in the Law and Prophets, as well as the Writings—what we call the Old Testament. Jesus never thought of himself as other than a Jew. This gives added depth to the adage of Pope Pius XII that all Christians are "spiritual Semites."

---

1. Alfred Plummer, *The Gospel according to St. Luke,* The International Critical Commentary (Edinburgh: T. and T. Clark, 1922, 1964), 62, in a note on Luke 2:21, states: "His (Jesus Christ) circumcision was a first step in His obedience to the will of God, and a first shedding of the redeeming blood. It was one of those things which became Him, in order 'to fulfill all righteousness' (Matthew, iii, 15). The contrast with the circumcision of the Baptist is marked. Here there is no family gathering of rejoicing neighbors and kinsfolk. Joseph and Mary are strangers in a village far from home."

2. Robert G. Hall, "Circumcision," *The Anchor Bible Dictionary,* vol. 1, ed. David Noel Freedman, (New York: Doubleday, 1992), 1026. Much of the material for this section is taken from this article, which runs from 1025–1032.

3. Matera, *Galatians,* 150: "born of a woman, born under the Law": Both phrases indicate the human condition of God's Son. The first uses a phrase employed elsewhere to describe the human condition (Job 14:1; Matthew 11:11); it neither implies nor denies the virgin birth. Although Paul may have known that the name of Jesus' mother was Mary, he does not refer to her by name in his writings. The second phrase *(hypo nomon)* is used in 3:23 and 4:5 to describe the situation of humanity's enslavement and in 5:18 it is contrasted with being led by the Spirit. Its use here indicates that God's Son experienced the fullness of the human condition.

Conclusion

༄

Whether Luke painted icons with pigments on wood and canvas, we do not know. But in his telling of the Nativity, he colors the Christian imagination. The images he evokes communicate a sense of reverence and awe with the mystery of God. With such a spirit of wonder, the shepherds spread the Good News:

> *When the angels had left them and gone into heaven, the shepherds said to one another, "Let us go now to Bethlehem and see this thing that has taken place, which the Lord has made known to us." So they went with haste and found Mary and Joseph, and the child lying in the manger. When they saw this, they made known what had been told them about this child; and all who heard it were amazed at what the shepherds told them. (Luke 2:15–18)*

El Greco Painted *The Adoration of the Shepherds*

El Greco (Domenikos Theotokopoulos, April 7, 1541–1614), the ancient master, painted *The Adoration of the Shepherds* around 1610. The picture is a reduced variant of an altarpiece painted before 1605 for Saint John of Ribera, patriarch of Antioch and archbishop of Valencia. El Greco made a habit of retaining reduced replicas of his paintings as part of his workshop inventory. In many cases these pictures were done by the workshop, but El Greco must have painted a great deal of the present picture. Indeed, the final result is substantially finer than the Valencia altarpiece.

In *The Adoration of the Shepherds*, the child (Jesus) is lying on a white wool blanket. At the foot of the manger is a white lamb with its legs tied, ready to be sacrificed.[1] The Virgin Mary and Joseph are on the right. Mary clasps the white wool blanket in her right hand and gently rests her left hand on it. Joseph is in a stance of adoration, both hands outstretched.

On the far right, Jesus Christ is standing, as distinct from his sitting position on the Mount of Olives, where he told the disciples about the appalling abomination and the distress of those days when,

> *The sun will be darkened,*
> *and the moon will not give its light;*
> *the stars will fall from heaven,*
> *and the powers of heaven will be shaken. (Matthew 24:29)[2]*

Four shepherds are depicted. In the foreground, El Greco prays with arms crossed over his heart. The donkey is behind El Greco and the ox in front of him:

> *The ox knows its owner,*
> *and the donkey its master's crib;*
> *but Israel does not know,*
> *my people do not understand. (Isaiah 1:3)*

High above are three cherubs, angels, holding a scroll on which part of their Christmas song is inscribed: GLOR(IA) IN EXC(ELSIS D)EO/HOMI(NIBUS)/LAVDAMUS TE BENEDICIMU(S TE).[3]

Luke paints a scene in his prologue that tells of the mission of Christ. Commentators are generally agreed that the original Lukan account of the Gospel began with chapter three. There, we have a formal beginning, akin to what now begins chapter one, and if we had no knowledge of the infancy narrative, we would think the Gospel complete:

> *In the fifteenth year of the reign of Emperor Tiberius, when*
> *Pontius Pilate was governor of Judea, and Herod was ruler of*
> *Galilee, and his brother Philip ruler of the region of Ituraea*

and Trachonitis, and Lysanias ruler of Abilene, during the high
priesthood of Annas and Caiaphas, the word of God came
to John son of Zechariah in the wilderness. (3:1–2)

Had Luke left his account with this beginning, it would have begun similarly to the Gospel according to Mark, which started with the baptism of Jesus by John the Baptist. That would not have seemed strange to us. Instead, Luke wrote a summary of the key theological themes that run through his account. The central concern of this prologue is to set forth the identity of Jesus in such a way that it would be engraved on the minds and hearts of his readers. Jesus was human, born of a woman, historically related to the biblical past, and enjoying normal human relationships to guide his maturation. Also divine, Jesus communicated the life of God to all who heard and accepted his word. The account appreciates the destiny of Jesus. He would return to the Father. This would come through suffering and pain. His disciples would not be bereft, for he would send his Spirit so that his work might continue in the Church—a story he tells in the Acts of the Apostles.

All of this Luke intimates in poetic fashion in the prologue. The more we read and reflect on it, the more we see and appreciate. At midnight Mass, a stillness comes over the assembly, as once again we hear the Christmas story. The images come rolling forth, one after another: Caesar Augustus issuing his decree, Joseph and Mary going from Nazareth to Bethlehem to be enrolled, the lack of hospitality in the city of David, Mary's giving birth, the swaddling, the manger, the angel, the heavenly choir, the appreciative shepherds. All of these engage our imagination, filling us with wonder and awe.

This awe should lead us to respond as did Mary, who treasured all these things and pondered them in her heart. Were they simply a list of historical facts, details in the beginning of a life lived two thousand years ago, they would not invite contemplation. But as poetic depictions of what will be spelled out in greater detail in the Gospel, they require prayerful reflection. They foreshadow the meaning of the rest of the Gospel account.

Perhaps, the detail that best exemplifies this is the introduction of the manger as the first crib for Jesus. That the manger is mentioned three times highlights its significance. Also underlining its importance is that we are told it is a sign. But a sign of what? It is a sign that, in this child, God finds a way to feed his people. Luke has in mind the history of the Church, and how Christ continues to be present to the members of his body, and the Eucharist that will enable us to recognize the living Christ in our midst.[4]

When we fail to penetrate the inner message in the Gospel according to Luke, we can take the *katalyma* (2:7) of Bethlehem as simply an inn, a place with hard-hearted owners refusing shelter to a pregnant woman. That is such a hard, cold fact. Luke, though, invites us to look further. He introduces the *katalyma* once again at the end of the life of Jesus as the guest room where Jesus ate the Passover with his disciples (22:11). Such a detail forces us to ask whether we are like Bethlehem in its lack of hospitality or whether Christ finds a welcome in our lives.

If we are open to pondering the mystery of the Incarnation, the Lukan account of the Gospel can help us realize whether we receive Jesus joyously as did the angels and shepherds. Such considerations of the mystery could aid our connecting the Incarnation with the celebration of the Eucharist, as did El Greco and the artists of the Cathedral of Chartres. El Greco suggested the coming Passion by painting a lamb with its legs tied, ready to be offered up in sacrifice. At the Cathedral of Chartres, the depictions of the Nativity show Jesus lying on an altar, enabling people in the Middle Ages to understand the inner meaning of the birth of Christ. God gives his firstborn Son as nourishment both at the Incarnation and the Eucharist.

May this book be just a beginning in your dwelling on the infancy narrative. With each reading of the prologue in Luke, we have a chance to delve deeper into the meaning of the Incarnation. In pondering the word of God, we may begin to realize the hospitality Jesus offers as he gives himself to us in the form of bread and wine. Jesus offers an infinite hospitality. It is the hospitality of a host forever beckoning guests to be nourished with the body and blood he has sacrificed for them. It is the hospitality of a Father who gave his Son to nourish the world. It is a hospitality that weaves together meal and sacrifice. The Eucharist, the sacrament that comes from this hospitality, never can be understood fully. But it must be pondered and treasured in our hearts. Such meditation surely will open our eyes ever wider to see Jesus "in the breaking of the bread" (Luke 24:35).

---

1. From Revelation 5:11–12: "Then I looked, and heard the voice of many angels surrounding the throne and the living creatures and the elders; they numbered myriads of myriads and thousands of thousands, singing with full voice,
   'Worthy is the Lamb that was slaughtered
   to receive power and wealth and wisdom and might
   and honor and glory and blessing!'"
   From the canticle in Isaiah 53:7:

   He was oppressed, and he was afflicted,
       yet he did not open his mouth;
   like a lamb that is led to the slaughter,
       and like a sheep that before its shearers is silent,
       so he did not open his mouth.

2. From Isaiah 13:10 and 13: "For the stars of the heaven and their constellations
   will not give their light;
   the sun will be dark at its rising,
       and the moon will not shed its light.

   Therefore I will make the heavens tremble,
       and the earth will be shaken out of its place,

at the wrath of the Lord of hosts
in the day of his fierce anger."

3. El Greco's *The Adoration of the Shepherds* celebrates God's praise: "Glory to God in the highest . . . . We praise thee, we bless thee (from the Great Doxology)."

4. One of the key Resurrection stories with which Luke ends his account of the Gospel is of the two disciples leaving Jerusalem to return home to Emmaus. Discouraged by Jesus' death, and not believing stories of the Resurrection, they are quitting the Christian community. The event that turned them back into disciples, proclaimers of the Gospel, is their encounter with Jesus, when they recognized him "in the breaking of the bread" (Luke 24:13–25). Theologically, Luke is telling us that the most intense experience we can have of the risen Lord in our lives is in the celebration of the Eucharist.